ONE + ONE

SCARVES, SHAWLS & SHRUGS

ONE + ONE

SCARVES, SHAWLS & SHRUGS

25+ PROJECTS FROM JUST TWO SKEINS

IRIS SCHREIER

LARK CRAFTS
Asheville

Editor
Valerie Van Arsdale Shrader

Assistant Editor
Thom O'Hearn

Art Director
Megan Kirby

Designer
Megan Kirby

Illustrator
Orrin Lundgren

Photographer
Lynne Harty

Cover Designer
Laura Palese

LARK CRAFTS

An Imprint of Sterling Publishing
387 Park Avenue South
New York, NY 10016

If you have questions or comments about
this book, please visit: larkcrafts.com

Library of Congress Cataloging-in-Publication Data

Schreier, Iris.

  One + one : scarves, shawls & shrugs : 25 projects from just two skeins / Iris Schreier.
    p. cm.
  ISBN 978-1-4547-0129-3
  1. Knitting—Patterns. I. Title. II. Title: One plus one : scarves, shawls & shrugs.
  TT825.S3927 2012
  746.43'2--dc23

            2011024215

10 9 8 7 6 5 4

Published by Lark Crafts
An Imprint of Sterling Publishing Co., Inc.
387 Park Avenue South, New York, NY 10016

Text © 2012, Iris Schreier
Photography © 2012, Lark Crafts, an Imprint of Sterling Publishing Co., Inc.
Illustrations © 2012, Lark Crafts, an Imprint of Sterling Publishing Co., Inc.

Distributed in Canada by Sterling Publishing, c/o Canadian Manda Group,
165 Dufferin Street, Toronto, Ontario, Canada M6K 3H6

Distributed in the United Kingdom by GMC Distribution Services,
Castle Place, 166 High Street, Lewes, East Sussex, England BN7 1XU

Distributed in Australia by Capricorn Link (Australia) Pty Ltd.,
P.O. Box 704, Windsor, NSW 2756 Australia

Manufactured in China

ISBN 13: 978-1-4547-0129-3

For information about custom editions, special sales, premium and corporate purchases, please
contact Sterling Special Sales Department at 800-805-5489 or specialsales@sterlingpub.com.

For information about desk and examination copies available to college and university professors,
requests must be submitted to academic@larkbooks.com. Our complete policy can be found at
www.larkcrafts.com.

contents

introduction

Have you ever entered a yarn shop and found it really difficult to choose between two lovely skeins of yarn? Now you can justify choosing both as you discover the joy of combining yarns to create beautiful, one-of-a-kind accessories. Often the sum of the two yarns is greater than the yarns individually. The One + One series focuses on two-skein projects that teach you how to mix yarns with optimal results. There are various ways to do this: Sometimes a yarn is made in two versions, one plain and one with embellishments like beads and sequins, or glitter. In other cases, different colors of the same yarn look incredibly beautiful together. You can also pair two dissimilar yarns, perhaps balancing an expensive luxury yarn with an equally beautiful (yet less dear) companion.

One + One: Scarves, Shawls & Shrugs features projects that run the gamut of neckwear, including scarves, shawls, shrugs, wraps, and cowls in different styles and silhouettes. And each one uses only two skeins of yarn, either in two colors of a single type of yarn or two completely different yarns.

Each lovely accessory helps you discover a different method for combining yarns. There are a number of unusual techniques to try, including lace, cables, modular, and slip-stitch knitting. You can also experiment with a wide range of colors and yarn types. In addition to the projects I created, I've included work from a dozen seasoned designers whose pieces offer their own unique perspectives.

Here's a sampling. Try the corrugated knitting technique in Cynthia Crescenzo's striped Corrugated Rib Scarf (page 36), which combines two different colors of the same yarn. Work part of a project with one yarn, then finish with a second yarn, as in Tanya Alpert's Exotic Draped Ruffle (page 25). Combine yarn weights like Lisa Hoffman did in her Flower Ruffle Keyhole Scarf (page 20), using a thicker yarn for the body and a lace weight for the flower edging. Integrate two different colors of a single yarn, as in Annie Modesitt's Slip Stitch Wimple (page 58).

Learn a unique short-row technique to create diamonds in my Diamond Lace Wrap (page 86), alternating yarn colors—or use short rows to create undulating rows, as in the Waves Stole (page 82). Continue to explore the use of color by emphasizing the interesting angles in a knitted piece, as in the Taj Mahal Scarf (page 32) or the Reverse Chevron Cowl (page 54). Alternate a thick-and-thin yarn to create the appearance of "floating stitches" in the Peekaboo Shrug (page 120).

Make your precious embellished yarn go a long way by alternating it with a plain yarn to create the large Mesh Wrap (page 94). Create a lovely cape with a beaded collar, following Laurie Kimmelstiel's Ruffled Collar Capelet (page 64) pattern. Use the embellished yarn as a trim to add weight and texture to the lightweight Cashmere Bolero (page 112) by Sharon Sorken.

The projects are suitable for all levels, from beginner to advanced, and the wide range of techniques offer many opportunities to add new skills to your repertoire. Before you begin, be sure to read through the Techniques chapter (page 122), to get a sense of how some of the stitch patterns and techniques are used. But most importantly, take what you can from this book, customize the patterns as you wish, and have lots of fun with it. I would love to see this as a launching point for your own interpretations and designs with just two skeins of yarn. Please share your project photos with me, either at www.facebook.com/artyarns or through this book's page on www.ravelry.com. And enjoy!

Team Scarf

materials and tools

Artyarns Cashmere 3 (100% cashmere; 1.8oz/50g = 170yd/155m): (A), 1 skein, color blue #226; (B), 1 skein, color pale green #301—approx 340yds/310m of fine-weight yarn;

Knitting needles: 4.0mm (size 6 U.S.) or size to obtain gauge

Cable needle

Tapestry needle

gauge

24 sts/32 rows – 4"/10cm in Stockinette Stitch

Always take time to check your gauge.

special abbreviations

C4F: Sl 2 sts to cable needle and hold in front, k2, k2 from cable needle

K1 f&b: Knit in the front and back of the same stitch

finished measurements

36" long x 5" wide/91cm x 13cm

Using one color in the ribbing and a different color for the cables leaves the flow of the cables uninterrupted. This neck warmer is perfect for all ages and both sexes; in cashmere it is absolutely scrumptious.

design by
Iris Schreier

skill level
intermediate

instructions

RIB PANEL

With A, CO 40 sts.

Row 1 (RS): K1, [k2, p2] 9 times, k3.

Row 2: K1, [p2, k2] 9 times, p2, k1.

Rows 3–48: Rep Rows 1 and 2.

Change to B.

CABLE PANEL 1

Row 1 (RS): K1 f&b, k3, p1, [k6, p1, k4, p1] 2 times, k6, p1, k3, k1 f&b—42 sts.

Row 2 and all even rows: K1, [p4, k1, p6, k1] 3 times, p4, k1.

Row 3: K1, [C4F, p1, C4F, k2, p1] 3 times, C4F, k1.

Row 5: K1, [C4F, p1, k2, C4F, p1] 3 times, C4F, k1.

Rows 7–34: Rep Rows 3–6.

CABLE PANEL 2

Row 1 (RS): K1, [C4F, p1, k2, p2, k2, p1] 3 times, C4F, k1.

Row 2: K1, [p4, k1, p1, k1, p2, k1, p1, k1] 3 times, p4, k1.

Row 3: K1, [C4F, p2, k4, p2] 3 times, C4F, k1.

Row 4: K1, [p4, k1, p2, k2, p2, k1] 3 times, p4, k1.

Row 5: K1, [C4F, p1, k1, p1, k2, p1, k1, p1] 3 times, C4F, k1.

Row 6: K1, [p4, k2, p4, k2] 3 times, p4, k1.

Rep Rows 1–6 eight times.

CABLE PANEL 3

Row 1: K1, [C4F, p2, k4, p2] 3 times, C4F, k1.

Row 2: K1, [p4, k1, p1, k1, p2, k1, p1, k1] 3 times, p4, k1.

Row 3: K1, [C4F, p1, k2, p2, k2, p1] 3 times, C4F, k1.

Row 4: K1, [p4, k2, p4, k2] 3 times, p4, k1.

Row 5: K1, [C4F, p1, k1, p1, k2, p1, k1, p1] 3 times, C4F, k1.

Row 6: K1, [p4, k1, p2, k2, p2, k1] 3 times, p4, k1.

Rep Rows 1–6 eight times.

Rep rows 1–34 of Cable Panel 1, dec 1 st each end of row on last row—40 sts. Change to A. Rep Rows 1–48 of Rib Panel. BO loosely.

FINISHING

Weave in ends. Block.

The technique used in this piece gives structure and detail to a normally soft and very drapey yarn. It's unusual yet fun to knit, and the intriguing method can be applied to any type of garment.

design by
Iris Schreier

skill level
intermediate

Romantic Jabot Collar

materials and tools

Artyarns Silk Pearl (100% silk; 1.8 oz/50g = 170yd/155m): (A), 1 skein, color khaki #H9—approx 170yd/155m of lightweight yarn;

Artyarns Beaded Pearl & Sequins (100% silk with glass beads and sequins, 1.8 oz/50g = 80 yd/73m): (B), 1 skein, color khaki #H9—approx 80 yd/73m of medium-weight yarn;

Knitting needles: 4.5mm (size 7 U.S.) or size to obtain gauge

Tapestry needle

gauge

16 sts/22 rows = 4"/10cm in Lace Pattern

Always take time to check your gauge.

special abbreviations

K1 f&b: Knit in the front and back of the same stitch

Inc2: Knit into the front and the back and the front of the same stitch

K3tog: Knit 3 sts together as though they were 1 stitch, a decrease of 2 sts

Turn: Transfer the left needle to the right hand and the right needle to the left hand, bringing the yarn up and over to the back between the tops of the 2 needles

Sl 1: Slip 1 stitch knitwise with yarn in back

finished measurements

45" long x 5" wide/97cm x 13cm

pattern stitches

NOTE: Each Triangle pattern is worked as a unit over 5 sts; complete all rows before moving to the next group of sts in the row.

TRIANGLE PATTERN— WORK PARTS 1 AND 2

PART 1. INCREASE
(starts with 5 sts)

K3, k1 f&b, k1, turn; sl 1, k1 f&b, k2, turn;

Sl 1, k1, k1 f&b, k3, turn; sl 1, k2, k1 f&b, k4, turn;

Sl 1, k3, k1 f&b, k5, turn; sl 1, k4, inc2, k6, turn.

PART 2. DECREASE
(ends with 5 sts)

Sl 1, k5, k3tog, k4, turn; sl 1, k3, k2tog, k4, turn;

Sl 1, k3, k2tog, k2, turn; sl 1, k1, k2tog, k2, turn;

Sl 1, ssk, k2tog, k2, do not turn.

LACE PATTERN
(worked over 25 sts)

Row 1 (RS): K1, [yo, s2kp, yo, k2] 4 times, yo, s2kp, yo, k1.

Row 2: K1, p to last st, k1.

Rep Rows 1 and 2 for pat.

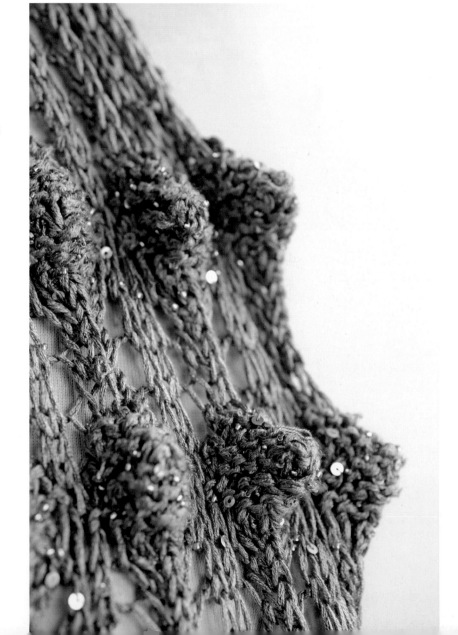

instructions

BOTTOM EDGING

With A, CO 25 sts.

Row 1 (RS): With B, work Triangle Pattern 5 times.

Row 2: Purl.

Row 3: With A, work Row 1 of Lace Pattern.

Row 4: With A, work Row 2 of Lace Pattern.

Rows 5–10: Rep Rows 3 and 4, carrying B loosely up the side of work, by twisting B over A. Change to B.

Rows 11–20: Rep Rows 1–10.

Rows 21–22: Rep Rows 1–2. Cut B.

SCARF BODY

With A, work in Lace Pat until piece measures 31"/79cm from beg.

TOP EDGING

Rep Bottom Edging. BO loosely.

FINISHING

Weave in ends. Block.

Flower Ruffle
Keyhole Scarf

materials and tools

Artyarns Cashmere Glitter (100% cashmere with Lurex; 1.8oz/
50g = 170yd/155m): (A), 1 skein, color white with silver #250s—
approx 170yd/155m of fine-weight yarn;

Artyarns Mohair Glitter (100% silk mohair with Lurex; 0.8oz/
25g = 312yd/285m): (B), 1 skein, color sage frost with silver #178s—
approx 310yd/283m of lace-weight yarn;

Knitting needles: 3.75mm (size 5 U.S.) or size to obtain gauge

Spare 3.75mm (size 5 U.S.) needle

Stitch holder

Tapestry needle

gauge

37 sts/27 rows = 4"/10cm in Faux Cable Pattern

Always take time to check your gauge.

special abbreviation

Turn: Transfer the left needle to the right hand and the right needle to
the left hand, bringing the yarn up and over to the back between the
tops of the 2 needles

finished measurements

23" long x 5½" wide/58cm x 14cm

This little scarf is soft
as a cloud and looks like a
carpet of glistening snow.
As an added surprise, twist
the ruffle after pulling it
through the keyhole and you
create a cool winter flower to
adorn your neck.

design by
Lisa Hoffman

skill level
intermediate
● ● ● ○

pattern stitch

FAUX CABLE
(multiple of 5 + 4 sts)

Row 1 (RS): Sl 1 kwise, *p2 tbl, k3; rep from * to last 3 sts, p2 tbl, k1.

Row 2: Sl 1 kwise, *k2 tbl, p3; rep from * to last 3 sts, end k2 tbl, k1.

Row 3: Sl 1 kwise, *p2 tbl, yo, k3, pull yo loosely over last 3 sts; rep from * to last 3 sts, end p2 tbl, k1.

Row 4: Rep Row 2.

Rep rows 1–4 for pat.

instructions

SCARF

With A, CO 54 sts.

Work in Faux Cable Pat until piece measures 20"/51cm, ending with Row 2.

DIVIDE FOR OPENING

Work first 27 sts as foll, place rem sts on holder.

Row 1 (RS): Sl 1 kwise, [p2 tbl, k3] 5 times, p1 tbl. Turn.

Row 2: K1 tbl, [p3, k2 tbl] 5 times, k1.

Row 3: Sl 1 kwise, [p2 tbl, yo, k3, pull yo over last 3 sts] 5 times, p1 tbl.

Row 4: Rep Row 2.

Rep rows 1–4 twice more, then work Rows 1 and 2 once. Place these sts on a holder and cut yarn leaving a 6"/15cm tail.

With RS facing, rejoin yarn to remaining sts and work as follows:

Row 1: P1 tbl, (k3, p2 tbl) 5 times, k1.

Row 2: Sl 1 kwise, [k2 tbl, p3] 5 times, k1 tbl. Turn.

Row 3: P1 tbl, [yo, k3, pull yo over last 3 sts, p2 tbl] 5 times, k1.

Row 4: Rep Row 2.

Rep Rows 1–4 twice more, then work Rows 1 and 2 once.

Fold in half with RS tog and join using 3-needle BO.

RUFFLE

With RS facing and B, pick up 52 sts along lower edge. Purl 1 row.

Row 1 (RS): K5, *p2, k3; rep from * to last 2 sts, k2.

Row 2: P5, *k2, p3; rep from * to last 2 sts, p2.

Row 3: K5, *M1, p2, M1, k3; rep from * to last 2 sts, k2—70 sts.

Row 4: P6, *k2, p5; rep from * to last st, k1.

Row 5: K6, *M1, p2, M1, k5; rep from * to last st, k1—88 sts.

Row 6: P7, *k2, p7; rep from * to end.

Row 7: K7, *M1, p2, M1, k7; rep from * across—106 sts.

Row 8: P8, *k2, p9; rep from *, end p8.

Row 9: K8, *M1, p2, M1, k9; rep from *, end k8—124 sts.

Row 10: P9, *k2, p11; rep from *, end p9.

Row 11: K9, *M1, p2, M1, k11; rep from *, end k9—142 sts.

Row 12 (turning row): Knit.

Row 13: K8, *k2tog, p2, k2tog, k9; rep from*, end k8—124 sts.

Row 14: P9, *k2, p11; rep from *, end p9.

Row 15: K7, *k2tog, p2, k2tog, k7; rep from * across—106 sts.

Row 16: P8, *k2, p9; rep from *, end p8.

Row 17: K6, *k2tog, p2, k2tog, k5; rep from * to last st, k1—88 sts.

Row 18: P7, *k2, p7; rep from * across.

Row 19: K5, *k2tog, p2, k2tog, k3; rep from * to last 2 sts, k2—70 sts.

Row 20: P6, *k2, p5; rep from * to last st, p1.

Row 21: K4, *k2tog, p2, k2tog, k1; rep from * to last 3 sts, k3—52 sts.

Row 22: P5, *k2, p3; rep from * to last 2 sts, p2.

Row 23: K5, *p2, k3; rep from * to last 2 sts, k2. BO.

FINISHING

Fold ruffle at turning row and seam BO edge to CO edge. Seam ends. Weave in ends. Block.

Exotic Draped Ruffle

materials and tools

Artyarns Regal Silk (100% silk; 1.8 oz/50g = 163yds/148m): (A), 1 skein, color peach #271—approx 163yds/148m of lightweight yarn;

Artyarns Beaded Mohair & Sequins (80% silk with glass beads and sequins, 20% mohair; 1.8oz/50g = 114yds/104m): (B), 1 skein, color peach #271G—approx 114yds/104m of lightweight yarn;

Knitting needles. 5.5mm (size 9 U.S.) or size to obtain gauge

Waste yarn

Tapestry needle

gauge

24 sts/20 rows = 4"/10cm in K1, P1 Rib Pattern

Always take time to check your gauge.

special abbreviation

M1 p-st: Make 1 purl st

finished measurements

50" long x 6½" wide/127cm x 17cm

This simple piece offers a combination of textures that give it a modern flare. The scarf can be worn to highlight either yarn—showing the silky side or the sparkly side.

design by
Tanya Alpert

skill level
beginner

instructions

FIRST HALF OF SCARF

With A, CO 40 sts using a provisional method. Change to B. Work in k1, p1 rib until piece measures 27"/69cm from beg.

RUFFLE

Change to A. Work in rib as set for 2 rows.

Row 1 (RS): *K1, M1, p1, rep from * across to last 2 sts, k2—59 sts.

Row 2: *P2, k1; rep from * to last 2 sts, p2.

Rows 3-4: Work even in pat.

Row 5: *K2, M1 p-st, p1, rep from * to last 2 sts, k2—78 sts.

Row 6: *P2, k2; rep from * to last 2 sts, p2.

Row 7: *K2, M1, p2; rep from * to last 2 sts, M1, k2—98 sts.

Row 8: *P3, k2; rep from * to last 3 sts, p3

Rows 9-10: Work even in pat.

Row 11: *K3, M1 p-st, p2, rep from * to last 3 sts, k3—117 sts.

Row 12: *P3, K3; rep from * to last 3 sts, p3. BO in pat.

SECOND HALF OF SCARF

Undo provisional CO and place live sts on needle. With A, work as for First Half until piece measures 18"/46cm from point where sts were joined. Work Ruffle as for First Half.

FINISHING

Weave in ends. Block.

Everything about this
design speaks of luxury
and opulence—especially
the embellished border.
This quick knit is full of
silkiness and shine.

design by
Iris Schreier

skill level
intermediate

Crown Royale Crescent

materials and tools

Artyarns Beaded Pearl & Sequins (100% silk with glass beads and sequins;
   1.8oz/50g = 80yd/73m): (A), 1 skein, color coral #H1—approx 80yd/73m
   of medium-weight yarn; 4

Artyarns Silk Pearl (100% silk; 1.8oz/50g = 170yd/155m): (B), 1 skein, color
   coral #H1—approx 170yd/155m of light-weight yarn; 3

Knitting needles: 5.0mm (size 8 U.S.) or size to obtain gauge

Tapestry needle

gauge

14 sts/26 rows = 4"/10cm in Garter Stitch

Always take time to check your gauge.

special technique

Wrap and turn: Work to indicated st, sl next st pwise, move yarn between
   needles, sl st back to left needle, move yarn back, turn (see Assorted
   Techniques, page 126)

finished measurements

49" wide x 12" deep/124cm x 30cm

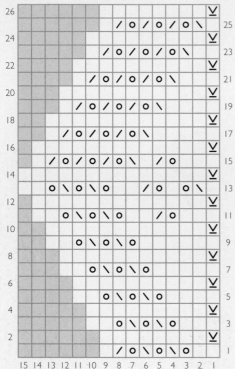

pattern chart

Chart legend:

⊻	sl 1 wyib
o	yo
＼	ssk
／	k2 tog
(blank)	knit on RS, purl on WS
(shaded)	no stitch

instructions

LACE BORDER
(worked over 9 sts)

With A, CO 9 sts.

Row 1 (RS): K2, [yo, ssk] twice, yo, k2tog, k1.

Row 2: P8, sl 1 wyib.

Row 3: K3, [yo, ssk] twice, yo, k2—10 sts.

Row 4: P9, sl 1 wyib.

Row 5: K4, [yo, ssk] twice, yo, k2—11 sts.

Row 6: P10, sl 1 wyib.

Row 7: K5, [yo, ssk] twice, yo, k2—12 sts.

Row 8: P11, sl 1 wyib.

Row 9: K6, [yo, ssk] twice, yo, k2—13 sts.

Row 10: P12, sl 1 wyib.

Row 11: K3, yo, k2tog, k2, [yo, ssk] twice, yo, k2—14 sts.

Row 12: P13, sl 1 wyib.

Row 13: K1, ssk, yo, k1, yo, k2tog, k2, [yo, ssk] twice, yo, k2—15 sts.

Row 14: P14, sl 1 wyib.

Row 15: K3, yo, k2tog, k1, ssk, [yo, k2tog] 3 times, k1—14 sts.

Row 16: P13, sl 1 wyib.

Row 17: K5, ssk, [yo, k2tog] 3 times, k1—13 sts.

Row 18: P12, sl 1 wyib.

Row 19: K4, ssk, [yo, k2tog] 3 times, k1—12 sts.

Row 20: P11, sl 1 wyib.

Row 21: K3, ssk, [yo, k2tog] 3 times, k1—11 sts.

Row 22: P10, sl 1 wyib.

Row 23: K2, ssk, [yo, k2tog] 3 times, k1—10 sts.

Row 24: P9, sl 1 wyib.

Row 25: K1, ssk, [yo, k2tog] 3 times, k1—9 sts.

Row 26: P8, sl 1 wyib.

Rep rows 1–26 eight more times. BO.

SHORT ROW SHAPING

With RS facing and B, pick up 117 sts along straight edge of border (1 in each slipped st) and purl back. Work short rows as follows, picking up all wraps and working them tog with st as you come to them:

K63, wrap and turn; p10, wrap and turn;

K15, wrap and turn; p20, wrap and turn;

K25, wrap and turn; p30, wrap and turn;

K35, wrap and turn; p40, wrap and turn;

K45, wrap and turn; p50, wrap and turn;

K55, wrap and turn; p60, wrap and turn;

K65, wrap and turn; p70, wrap and turn;

K75, wrap and turn; p80, wrap and turn;

K85, wrap and turn; p90, wrap and turn;

K95, wrap and turn; p100, wrap and turn;

K105, wrap and turn; p110, wrap and turn;

Work 2 more rows in St st, picking up wraps.

TOP EDGE

Row 1 (RS): BO 10, [k1, p1] across to end.

Repeat Row 1 three more times— 77 sts. BO.

FINISHING

Weave in ends. Block.

Like its namesake, the lovely symmetrical yet angular peaks of this scarf have a Zen-like peaceful quality. Work this piece with two drastically different yarns in two different colorways, one solid and one variegated.

**design by
Iris Schreier**

**skill level
intermediate**

Taj Mahal Scarf

materials and tools

Artyarns Silk Pearl (100% silk; 1.8oz/50g = 170yd/155m): (A), 1 skein, color multi #171 —approx 170yd/155m of lightweight yarn;

Artyarns Cashmere 5 (100% cashmere; 1.8oz/50g = 102yd/93m): (B), 1 skein, color red #244—approx 102yd/93m of medium-weight yarn;

Knitting needles: 5.0mm (size 8 U.S.) or size to obtain gauge

Stitch markers

Stitch holders

Tapestry needle

gauge

20 sts/36 rows = 4"/10cm in Garter Stitch

Always take time to check your gauge.

special abbreviation

K1 f&b: Knit in the front and back of the same stitch

finished measurements

44" long x 5" wide/112cm x 13cm

instructions

SCARF HALF
(make 2)

With A, CO 3 sts.

Row 1: K1, k1 f&b, k1—4sts.

Row 2: K1 f&b, k1 f&b, PM, k2—6 sts.

Row 3: K1 f&b, k to marker, remove marker, k1 f&b, PM, k to end—8 sts.

Rep Row 3 until there are 28 sts.

BODY

Row 1: K to marker, remove marker, k1 f&b, PM, (k2, k2tog, k1 f&b) twice, k2, k2tog.

Row 2: Rep Row 1. Change to B.

Rep Row 1 twice more. Cont to rep Row 1, following color sequence as follows: 4 rows A, 2 rows B, 6 rows A, 4 rows B, 6 rows A, 2 rows B. Carry unused yarn along edge, twisting it around working yarn to prevent long loops. Cont as set until piece measures approx 22"/56cm. Place sts on holder.

FINISHING

NOTE: *Scarf halves are joined by working triangles between them on each side.*

On the second half of the scarf, leave the 14 sts farthest from the working yarn on the holder, place the first 14 sts on the needle. Place the 14 sts farthest from the working yarn from the first half on the needle, leave rem 14 sts on holder—28 sts. Alternate A and B every 2 rows throughout.

Row 1 (RS): K12, k2tog, PM, k12, k2tog—26 sts.

Row 2: K to 1 st before marker, remove marker, k2tog, PM, k to last 2 sts, k2tog—24 sts.

Rep Row 2 until 4 sts rem.

Next Row: K2tog, k2tog—2 sts.

Next Row: K2tog—1 st. Fasten off.

Rep on opposite side.

Weave in ends. Block.

The intriguing rib pattern creates a fabric that's doubly thick, resulting in an incredibly warm yet lightweight garment with a woven look. The design is unisex and the yarn choices can be personalized for a man or a woman.

design by
Cynthia A. Crescenzo

Corrugated Rib Scarf

materials and tools

Artyarns Cashmere 5 (100% cashmere; 1.8oz/50g = 102yd/93m): (A), 1 skein, color tonal brown #2293; (B), 1 skein, color antique cream #H14—approx 204 yds/186m of medium-weight yarn; (4)

Knitting needles: 6.5mm (size 10½ U.S.) or size to obtain gauge

Tapestry needle

gauge

24 sts and 24 rows = 4"/10cm

Always take time to check your gauge.

finished measurements

Approx 42" long x 4¾" wide/107cm x 11cm, after blocking

pattern stitch

CORRUGATED RIB
(over an even number of sts)

Row 1 (RS): *With A, k1. Leave A in back. Bring B forward between the needles and p1. Move B between the two needles to back; repeat from * to end of row.

Repeat from * to end of row.

Row 2: *With B, k1. Bring B forward between the needles. With A, p1. Leave A in front, move B to the back between the needles; repeat from * to end of row. Rep Rows 1 and 2 for pat.

NOTE: *Move yarn between needles to WS after st is complete as needed; do not strand yarn across RS of work.*

instructions

SCARF

With A, CO 30 sts. Purl 1 row. Work in
  Corrugated Rib Pat until piece measures 41"/104cm, ending with Row 2.

Next row (RS): With A, purl. BO
  loosely.

FINISHING

Weave in ends. Block.

Lacy Textured Cowl

materials and tools

Artyarns Ensemble Light (60% silk, 40% cashmere; 3.5oz/100g
= 400yd/366m): (A), 1 skein, color goldenrod #H12—approx
400yd/366m of lightweight yarn;

Artyarns Cashmere 1 (100% cashmere; 1.8oz/50g = 510yd/466m):
(B), 1 skein, color goldenrod #H12—approx 400yd/366m of lace-
weight yarn;

Knitting needles: 4mm (size 6 U.S.) 24"/61cm circular needles or size to
obtain gauge

Cable needle

Stitch marker

Tapestry needle

2½"/6cm piece of cardboard

gauge

18 sts/24 rows = 4"/10cm using A in Open Cable Stitch

Always take time to check your gauge.

special abbreviation

C8F: Sl 4 sts to cable needle and hold in front, k4, k4 from cable needle

finished measurements

32" circumference x 13" high/81cm x 23cm, after blocking

Knit in an open cable stitch, this piece becomes a great textural accessory. You can stretch it along your shoulders, wear it scrunched up around your neck, gather it up with the drawstring, or leave it open—many options to play with.

design by
Laura Zukaite

skill level
intermediate

pattern stitch

OPEN CABLE STITCH PATTERN
(multiple of 16 sts)

Rounds 1 and 3: *K8, p8; rep from * around.

Round 2: *K8, yo, p2tog, p4, p2tog, yo; rep from * around.

Round 4: *C8F, yo, p2tog, p4, p2tog, yo; rep from * around.

Rounds 5 and 7: Rep Rnd 1.

Rounds 6 and 8: Rep Rnd 2. Rep Rnds 1–8 for pat.

instructions

COWL

With B, CO 144 sts. PM and join, being careful not to twist. Knit 2 rnds. Work Rnds 1–8 of Open Cable Stitch Pat once. Cont in pat, changing yarns as follows:

Round 1: Work in A.

Rounds 2–3: Work in B.

Rounds 4–5: Work in A.

Round 6: Work in B.

Rounds 7–8: Work in A.

Work in A until piece measures 12"/30cm from beg, ending with Rnd 8 of pat.

Cont in pat, changing yarns as follows:

Round 1: Work in B.

Rounds 2–3: Work in A.

Rounds 4–5: Work in B.

Round 6: Work in A.

Rounds 7–8: Work in B.

With B, work Rnds 1–8 once more. Knit 2 rnds. BO loosely.

FINISHING

Weave in ends. Block.

TWISTED CORD

Cut a strand of A approx 2yd/2m long. Fold in half and anchor to doorknob. Twist strands clockwise until they start to kink and fold up on themselves; allow to fold in half again. Secure ends, trim. Cord should measure approx 26"/66cm.

TASSELS
(make 2)

Wrap A around 2 1/2"/6cm piece of cardboard to sufficient thickness. Thread strand of yarn under top edge of tassel and tie. Slide off cardboard and tie around tassel approx 1/2"/1cm down from top. Cut loops at bottom of tassel.

Attach a tassel to one end of twisted cord. Weave cord through eyelets on side of center front cable, then down through eyelets on opposite side. Attach tassel to opposite end of cord. Pull to gather.

This cowl is a great way to
try cabling for the first time
because it is performed in
a series of easy steps. The
flowers at either end provide
the perfect edge for this
funky neckpiece.

design by
Michelle Miller

skill level
intermediate

Easy Cable Cowl

materials and tools

Artyarns Ultrabulky (100% merino wool; 3.5oz/100g = 110yd/101m):
(A), 1 skein, color blue #304; (B), 1 skein, color tonal blue #2304—
approx 220yds/202m of bulky-weight yarn; **5**

Knitting needles: 9mm (size 13 U.S.) or size to obtain gauge

Cable needle

Tapestry needle

gauge

15 sts/13 rows = 4"/10cm in Cable Pattern with A and B held tog

Always take time to check your gauge.

special abbreviations

T5B: Sl 2 sts to cable needle and hold in back, k3, p2 from cable needle

T5F: Sl 3 sts to cable needle and hold in front, p2, k3 from cable needle

finished measurements

24" circumference x 6" deep/61cm x 15cm

pattern chart

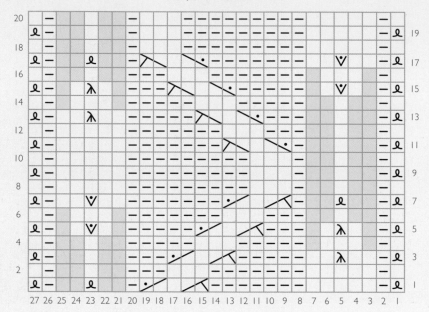

♀		k1tbl
−		purl on WS, knit on RS
		knit on RS, purl on WS
⋅╱ ╲		T5B
		no stitch
λ		sk2p
V		(k1,p1,k1) in 1 st
╲ ╱⋅		T5F

pattern stitch

CABLE
(worked over 23 sts)

Row 1 (RS): K1 tbl, p1, k5, p7, T5B, p1, k1 tbl, p1, k1 tbl—23 sts.

Row 2: P1, k1, p1, k3, p3, k7, p5, k1, p1.

Row 3: K1 tbl, p1, k1, s2kp, k1, p5, T5B, p3, k1 tbl, p1, k1 tbl—21 sts.

Row 4: P1, k1, p1, k5, p3, k5, p3, k1, p1.

Row 5: K1 tbl, p1, sk2p, p3, T5B, p5, [k1, p1, k1] in same st, p1, k1 tbl.

Row 6: P1, k1, p3, k7, p3, k3, p1, k1, p1.

Row 7: K1 tbl, p1, k1 tbl, p1, T5B, p7, k1, [k1, p1, k1] in same st, k1, p1, k1 tbl—23 sts.

Row 8: P1, k1, p5, k9, p3, k1, p1, k1, p1.

Row 9: K1 tbl, p1, k1, p1, k3, p9, k5, p1, k1 tbl.

Row 10: P1, k1, p5, k9, p3, k1, p1, k1, p1.

Row 11: K1 tbl, p1, k1, p1, T5F, p7, k5, p1, k1 tbl.

Row 12: P1, k1, p5, k7, p3, k3, p1, k1, p1.

Row 13: K1 tbl, p1, k1, p3, T5F, p5, k1, sk2p, k1, p1, k1 tbl—21 sts.

Row 14: P1, k1, p3, k5, p3, k5, p1, k1, p1.

Row 15: K1 tbl, p1, [k1, p1, k1] into same st, p5, T5F, p3, sk2p, p1, k1.

Row 16: P1, k1, p1, k3, p3, k7, p3, k1, p1.

Row 17: K1 tbl, p1, k1, [k1, p1, k1] into same st, k1, p7, T5F, p1, k1 tbl, p1, k1 tbl—23 sts.

Row 18: P1, k1, p1, k1, p3, k9, p5, k1, p1.

Row 19: K1 tbl, p1, k5, p9, k3, p1, k1, p1, k1 tbl.

Row 20: P1, k1, p1, k1, p3, k9, p5, k1, p1.

Rep rows 1–20 for pat.

instructions

COWL

With A and B held tog, CO 23 sts. Purl 1 row. Rep Rows 1–20 of Cable Pat a total of 4 times. BO.

FINISHING

Seam. Weave in ends. Block.

Diamond Spiral

materials and tools

Artyarns Ultrabulky (100% merino wool; 3.5oz/100g = 110yd/101m): (A), 1 skein, color indigo #303; (B), 1 skein, color pinks #H1—approx 220yds/202m0bulky-weight yarn;

Knitting needles: 5.5mm (size 9 U.S.) 24"/61cm circular needle or size to obtain gauge

Stitch marker

Tapestry needle

gauge

12 sts/24 rows = 4"/10cm in Garter Stitch

Always take time to check your gauge.

special abbreviations

K1 f&b: Knit in the front and back of the same stitch

Sl 1: Slip 1 knitwise with yarn in back

Turn: Transfer the left needle to the right hand and the right needle to the left hand, bringing the yarn up and over to the back between the tops of the 2 needles

finished measurements

54" circumference x 5" wide/137cm x 13cm

This twisted cowl was inspired by a magazine photo of a houndstooth scarf in two bold colors. It is knitted in the round using a faux entrelac technique that makes it reversible. It's a quick knit in a bulky yarn.

design by
Iris Schreier

skill level
intermediate

pattern stitches

NOTE: Each pat is worked as a unit; complete all rows before moving to next group of sts indrnd.

BEGINNING TRIANGLE PATTERN
(worked over 5 sts, inc to 10 sts)

K1 f&b, turn; sl 1, turn;

K1 f&b, k1, turn; sl 1, k1, turn;

K1 f&b, k2, turn; sl 1, k2, turn;

K1 f&b, k3, turn; sl 1, k3, turn;

K1 f&b, k4, do not turn.

DIAMOND PATTERN
(worked over 10 sts):

[K1 f&b, k3, ssk, turn; sl 1, k4, turn] 4 times;

K1 f&b, k3, ssk, do not turn.

ENDING TRIANGLE PATTERN
(worked over 10 sts, dec to 5 sts):

K4, ssk, turn; sl 1, k3, turn;

Sl 1, k2, ssk, turn; sl 1, k2, turn;

Sl 1, k1, ssk, turn; sl 1, k1, turn;

Sl 1, ssk, turn; sl 1, turn;

Ssk, do not turn.

instructions

COWL

With A, CO 120 sts. Change to B.

Round 1: With B, work Beginning Triangle Pattern 24 times. PM and join, deliberately twisting needles once before joining to create a moebius.

Round 2: With A, work Diamond Pattern 24 times.

Round 3: With B, rep round 2.

Rounds 4-5: Rep rounds 2-3.

Round 6: With A, work Ending Triangle Pattern 24 times. BO loosely.

FINISHING

Weave in ends. Block.

Infinity Twist

materials and tools

Artyarns Silk Rhapsody Glitter Light (68% silk, 32% mohair with metallic; 2.8oz/80g = 400yd/238m): (A), 1 skein, color multi #1015—approx 400yd/238m of lightweight yarn,

Artyarns Ultramerino 4 (100% merino wool; 1.8oz /50g = 191yd/ 175m). (B), 1 skein, color green #297—approx 191yd/175m of lace-weight yarn;

Knitting needles: 3.75mm (size 5 U.S.) or size to obtain gauge

Crochet hook: 3.75mm (size F-5 U.S.)

Tapestry needle

gauge

28 sts/32 rows = 4"/10cm in K1, P1 Rib Pattern using A

Always take time to check your gauge.

finished measurements

86" circumference x 6" wide/218cm x 15cm

This versatile piece offers an array of luscious areas of color in a continuous loop, long enough to envelop your neck three times. It works double duty as a scarf and a cowl.

design by
Judith Rudnick Kane

skill level
beginner

instructions

COWL

With A, CO 42 sts.

Row 1: With A, *k1, p1; rep from * across.

Rows 2-3: With B, knit.

Rows 4-7: With A, rep Row 1.

Rep Rows 2–7 until B is used up. Work
Row 1 once more. BO loosely.

FINISHING

Twist once and seam ends, creating a
Möbius loop.

With crochet hook and A, work 1 round
of single crochet around outside
edges. Weave in ends. Block.

The zigs and zags in this design make for some interesting knitting; use two high-contrast colors and yarns to maximize the effect. This delightful piece can be worn in many different ways.

design by
Iris Schreier

skill level
intermediate

Reverse Chevron Cowl

materials and tools

Artyarns Beaded Silk (100% silk with glass beads; 1.8oz/50g = 160yd/146m): (A), 1 skein, color black with black beads #246M—approx 160yd/146m of lightweight yarn; (3)

Artyarns Silk Pearl (100% silk; 1.8oz/50g = 170yd/155m): (B), 1 skein, color tonal brown #3248—approx 170yd/155m of lightweight yarn; (3)

Knitting needles: 4.5mm (size 7 U.S.) or size to obtain gauge

Stitch markers

Tapestry needle

gauge

20 sts/32 rows = 4"/10cm in Garter Stitch

Always take time to check your gauge.

special abbreviation

K1 f&b: Knit in the front and back of the same stitch

finished measurements

34" circumference x 7½" wide/86cm x 19cm

pattern stitches

RIB SIDE 1
(worked over 5 sts)
K1, p1, k1, p1, k1.

RIB SIDE 2
(worked over 5 sts)
P1, k1, p1, k1, p1.

CHEVRON 1
(worked over 18 sts)
K8, k1 f&b, k7, k2tog.

CHEVRON 2
(worked over 18 sts)
K1 f&b, k7, k2tog, k8.

instructions

COWL

With A, CO 51 sts. PM after sts 5, 23, 28, and 46 to mark panel transitions. The markers will be sl throughout.

Row 1: With A, work Rib Side 1 over 5 sts, work Chevron 1 over 18 sts, work Rib Side 1 over 5 sts, work Chevron 2 over 18 sts, work Rib Side 1 over 5 sts.

Row 2: With A, work Rib Side 2 over 5 sts, work Chevron 2 over 18 sts, work Rib Side 2 over 5 sts, work Chevron 1 over 18 sts, work Rib Side 2 over 5 sts.

Rows 3–8: With B, rep Rows 1–2, carrying A loosely up the side.

Rep Rows 1–8 until piece measures 34"/86cm. BO.

FINISHING

Seam. Weave in ends. Block.

Slip Stitch Wimple

Only one color at a time is used in this interesting slip-stitch pattern that mimics a more complicated stranded-knit project. The piece can be worn several ways: as a hat with the ribbing drawn together at the top of the head, as a headband, or pulled down as a "turtleneck" cowl.

design by
Annie Modesitt

skill level
intermediate

materials and tools

Artyarns Ultrabulky (100% merino wool; 3.5oz/100g = 110yd/101m): (A), 1 skein, color black/grey #148; (B), 1 skein, color red oranges #299— approx 220yds/202m of bulky-weight yarn; (5)

Knitting needles: 6.5mm (size 10½ U.S.) 16"/41cm circular needle or size to obtain gauge

Stitch marker

Tapestry needle

gauge

15 sts/22 rows = 4"/10cm in Stockinette Stitch

Always take time to check your gauge.

finished measurements

21" circumference x 13" long/53cm x 33cm

pattern stitch

SLIP STITCH
(multiple of 4 sts)
Rounds 1-2: With B, knit.
Round 3: With A, *sl 1, k1; rep from * around.
Round 4: With A, purl.
Round 5: With B, knit.
Round 6: With A, *sl 1, k1; rep from * around.
Round 7: With A, knit.
Round 8: With B, *k1, sl 1; rep from * around.
Round 9: With A, purl.
Round 10: With B, *K1, sl 1; rep from * around.
Rounds 11-12: With B, knit.

instructions

COWL

With A, CO 80 sts. PM and join, being careful not to twist. Work in k2, p2 rib for 1½"/4cm. Work Rnds 1–4 of Slip Stitch Pat once, then rep Rnds 5–8 until piece measures 6"/15cm from beg. Work Rnds 9–12 once. Change to k2, p2 rib and work in B for 12 rounds, then A for 12 rounds, then B for 2 rounds, then A for 1 round, then B for 6 rounds. BO loosely in pat.

FINISHING

Weave in ends. Block.

Beaded Neckwarmer

materials and tools

Artyarns Silk Pearl (100% silk; 1.8oz/50g = 170yd/155m): (A), 1 skein, color red #295—approx 170yds/155m of lightweight yarn;

Artyarns Beaded Pearl (100% silk with glass beads; 1.8oz/50g = 100yd/91m): (B), 1 skein, color red #295—approx 100yds/91m of medium-weight yarn;

Knitting needles: 3.75mm (size 5 U.S.) 24"/61cm circular needle or size to obtain gauge

Stitch marker

Tapestry needle

gauge

26 sts/30 rows = 4"/10cm in Lace Pattern

Always take time to check your gauge.

finished measurements

18" circumference x 12" wide/46cm x 30cm

Add a little jeweled drama to your look with this light and drapey cowl. By alternating the yarns in an intriguing lace, the cowl appears to be beaded throughout even though one yarn is not.

design by
Lisa Hoffman

skill level
easy

pattern stitches

GARTER BORDER
(worked over any number of sts)

Round 1: Knit.

Round 2: Purl.

Round 3: Knit.

LACE PATTERN
(multiple of 7 sts)

Round 1: *K1, yo, p1, p3tog, p1, yo, k1;
rep from * around.

Round 2: Knit.

Rep Rnds 1 and 2 for pat.

instructions

COWL

With A, loosely CO 119 sts. Place
marker and join, being careful not
to twist. Work Rnds 1–3 of Garter
Border, then beg Lace Pattern, alt 1
rnd of A with 1 rnd of B throughout,
until piece measures 11¾"/30cm
from beg, ending with Rnd 2.
Change to A. Work Rnds 2–3 of
Garter Border once more. BO
loosely.

FINISHING

Weave in ends. Block.

This little capelet has a vintage look, with its ruffled collar edging and an i-cord tie. It is perfect to throw on over a classic sleeveless dress or just accessorize any summery top or evening outfit.

design by
Laurie Kimmelstiel

skill level
intermediate

Ruffled Collar Capelet

materials and tools

Artyarns Ensemble (75% silk, 25% cashmere; 3.5oz/100g = 256yd/234m): (A), 1 skein, color light blue #307—approx 256yd/234m of medium-weight yarn; (4)

Artyarns Beaded Ensemble (85% silk with glass beads, 15% cashmere with metallic thread; 3.5oz/100g = 125yd/110m): (B), 1 skein, color light blue #307—approx 125yd/110m of medium-weight yarn; (4)

Knitting Needles: 3.75mm (size 5 U.S.) 24"/61cm circular needle, 4.5mm (size 7 U.S.) 24"/61cm circular and set of 2 dpns or size to obtain gauge

Stitch markers

Tapestry needle

gauge

18 sts/28 rows = 4"/10cm in St st using smaller needles and A

16 sts/28 rows = 4"/10cm in St st using larger needles and B

Always take time to check your gauge.

special abbreviations

K1 f&b: Knit in the front and back of the same stitch

finished measurements

Approx 28"/71cm neck circumference x 11"/28cm deep

pattern stitch

SEED STITCH
(over 3 sts at each edge)
Row 1: P1, k1, p1.
Rep row 1 for pat.

NOTE: Capelet is worked from the top down. Slip markers as you come to them throughout.

instructions

BODY

With smaller needles and A, CO 105 sts.

Row 1 (RS): Seed Stitch over 3 sts, PM, knit to last 3 sts, PM, Seed Stitch to end.

Row 2 and all even rows: Seed Stitch over 3 sts, purl to last 3 sts, Seed Stitch to end.

Row 3: Rep row 1.

Row 5: Row 5: Seed Stitch as set, slip marker, k1 f&b, *k13, k1 f&b, PM; rep from * to last 3 sts, slip marker, Seed Stitch—113 sts.

Work even for 3 rows.

Next Row (inc row): Seed Stitch as set, *knit to 1 st before next marker, k1 f&b; rep from * to last 3 sts, Seed Stitch—8 sts inc.

Work even for 3 rows. Rep from ** until there are 201 sts. Work even until piece measures approx 10"/25cm, ending with a WS row. Change to B.

Next Row (RS): Seed Stitch as set, *k4, k1 f&b; rep from * to last 3 sts, removing all markers except those at ends, Seed Stitch—240 sts. Work even for 3 rows.

Next Row (RS): Seed Stitch as set, *k5, M1, k1, M1; rep from * to last 3 sts, Seed Stitch—318 sts. Work even for 2 rows. BO.

COLLAR

With RS facing, larger needles and B, pick up 105 sts along top edge.

Row 1 (RS of collar): [K1 f&b] twice, knit to last 2 sts, [k1 f&b] twice—109 sts.

Row 2 and all even rows: K1, purl to last st, k1.

Row 3: [K1 f&b] 3 times, knit to last 3 sts, [k1 f&b] 3 times—115 sts.

Row 5: K1, [k1 f&b] 3 times, knit to last 4 sts, [k1 f&b] 3 times, k1—121 sts.

Row 7: K1, k1 f&b, knit to the last 2 sts, k1 f&b, k1—123 sts.

Rows 8-14: Work even.

Row 15: K1, *k2, k1 f&b; rep from * to last 2 sts, k2—163 sts.

Row 17: Rep Row 15, beg and ending with k2—216 sts.

FINISHING

Weave in ends. Block.

TIES (make 2)

With dpns and B, CO 3 sts. Work in I-cord for 10"/25cm. BO, leaving an 8"/20cm tail. Sew ties to neck edge openings beneath the collar.

Lavish Cape

materials and tools

Art Yarns Silk Rhapsody (50% silk, 50% kid mohair; 3.5oz/100g = 260yd/238m): (A), 1 skein, color leaf green #2217—approx 260yd/234m of medium-weight yarn;

Art Yarns Silk Rhapsody Glitter (80% silk, 20% mohair w/ metallic; 3.5oz/100g = 260yd/238m): (B), 1 skein, color leaf green #2217—approx 260yd/234m of medium weight yarn;

Knitting needles. 5.0mm (size 8 U.S.) 32"/81cm circular needles and 4.0mm (size 6 U.S.) 24"/61cm circular needles, or size to obtain gauge

Tapestry needle

gauge

16 sts/22 rows = 4"/10cm using larger needles and A

Always take time to check your gauge.

special abbreviation

P1 f&b: Purl in the front and back of the same stitch

finished measurements

Approx 17" neck circumference x 15" deep/43cm x 38cm

For sheer romance, it's hard to surpass this beautiful piece. The metallic yarn adds shimmer, while the silk/mohair blend offers substance.

design by
Brooke Nico

instructions

NECK EDGE

With smaller needles and A, CO 69 sts.

Row 1 (RS): K2, *p1, k1; rep from * across, end k2.

Row 2: P2, *k1, p1; rep from * across, end p2.

Rows 3–6: Rep Rows 1 and 2.

Row 7: K2, *work (p1, k1) in next st, k1; rep from * across, end p1, k2—101 sts.

Row 8: P2, *k1, p2; rep from * across, end k1, p2.

Row 9: K2, *p1, k2; rep from * across, end p1, k2.

Row 10: Rep Row 8.

Row 11: K2, *p1 f&b, k10, yo, k1, yo; rep from * across, end p1 f&b, k2—126 sts.

Row 12: P2, *k2, p13; rep from * across, end k2, p2.

LACE PATTERN

Change to larger needles. Each RS row begins k2 and ends p2, k2; pat rep is worked 8 times across. Chart shows pat rep only.

Row 1 (RS): K2, *p2, k9, k3tog, yo, k1, yo; rep from * across, end p2, k2.

Row 2 and all even rows: Work sts as they appear.

Row 3: K2, *p2, k7, k3tog, k1, yo, k1, yo, k1; rep from * across, end p2, k2.

Row 5: K2, *p2, k5, k3tog, k2, yo, k1, yo, k2; rep from * across, end p2, k2.

Row 7: K2, *p2, k3, k3tog, k3, yo, k1, yo, k3; rep from * across, end p2, k2.

Row 9: K2, *p2, yo, k1, yo, sk2p, k9; rep from * across, end p2, k2.

Row 11: K2, *p2, k1, yo, k1, yo, k1, sk2p, k7; rep from * across, end p2, k2.

Row 13: K2, *p2, k2, yo, k1, yo, k2, sk2p, k5; rep from * across, end p2, k2.

Row 15: K2, *p2, k3, yo, k1, yo, k3, sk2p, k3; rep from * across, end p2, k2.

Row 17: K2, *p2, k4, yo, k1, yo, k4, k3tog, yo, k1, yo; rep from * across, end p2, k2—142 sts.

Row 19: K2, *p2, k9, k3tog, k1, yo, k1, yo, k1; rep from * across, end p2, k2.

Row 21: K2, *p2, k7, k3tog, k2, yo, k1, yo, k2; rep from * across, end p2, k2.

Row 23: K2, *p2, k5, k3tog, k3, yo, k1, yo, k3; rep from * across, end p2, k2.

Row 25: K2, *p2, k3, k3tog, k4, yo, k1, yo, k4; rep from * across, end p2, k2.

Row 27: K2, *p2, yo, k1, yo, sk2p, k5, yo, k1, yo, k5; rep from * across, end p2, k2—158 sts.

Row 29: K2, *p2, k1, yo, k1, yo, k1, sk2p, k11; rep from * across, end p2, k2.

Row 31: K2, *p2, k2, yo, k1, yo, k2, sk2p, k9; rep from * across, end p2, k2.

Row 33: K2, *p2, k3, yo, k1, yo, k3, sk2p, k7; rep from * across, end p2, k2.

Row 35: K2, *p2, k4, yo, k1, yo, k4, sk2p, k5; rep from * across, end p2, k2.

Row 37: K2, *p2, k5, yo, k1, yo, k5, sk2p, k3; rep from * across, end p2, k2.

Row 39: K2, *p2, k6, yo, k1, yo, k6, k3tog, yo, k1, yo; rep from * across, end p2, k2—174sts.

Row 41: K2, *p2, k13, k3tog, k1, yo, k1, yo, k1; rep from * across, end p2, k2.

Row 43: K2, *p2, k11, k3tog, k2, yo, k1, yo, k2; rep from * across, end p2, k2.

Row 45: K2, *p2, k9, k3tog, k3, yo, k1, yo, k3; rep from * across, end p2, k2.

Row 47: K2, *p2, k7, k3tog, k4, yo, k1, yo, k4; rep from * across, end p2, k2.

Row 49: K2, *p2, k5, k3tog, k5, yo, k1, yo, k5; rep from * across, end p2, k2.

Row 51: K2, *p2, k3, k3tog, k6, yo, k1, yo, k6; rep from * across, end p2, k2.

Row 53: K2, *p2, k1, k3tog, k7, yo, k1, yo, k7; rep from * across, end p2, k2.

Row 55: K2, *p2, k2tog, k8, yo, k1, yo, k8; rep from * across, end p2, k2—182 sts.

Row 57: K2, *p1, p2tog tbl, k9, yo, k1, yo, k9; rep from * across, end p2, k2—190 sts.

Change to B.

pattern chart

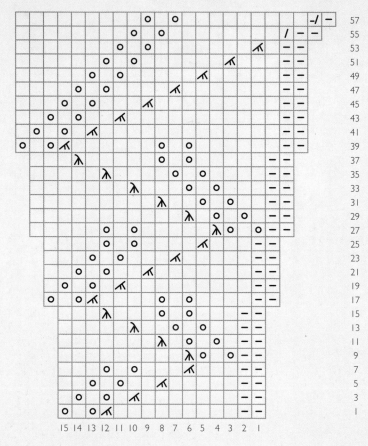

☐	knit on RS, purl on RS
−	purl on RS, knit on WS
o	yo
λ	sk2p
⋏	k3tog
-/	p2tog tbl
/	k2tog

EDGING

Row 59: K2, *k2tog, yo, ssk, k17, k2tog, yo; rep from * across, end k2tog, k2—181 sts.

Row 60 and all even rows: Purl.

Row 61: K2, *k1, yo, k1, yo, ssk, k15, k2tog, yo, k1, yo; rep from * across, end k3—197 sts.

Row 63: K2, *k1, yo, k1, [yo, ssk] 2 times, k13, [k2tog, yo] 2 times, k1, yo; rep from * across, end k3—213 sts.

Row 65: K2, *k1, yo, k1, [yo, ssk] 3 times, k11, [k2tog, yo] 3 times, k1, yo; rep from * across, end k3—229 sts.

Row 67: K2, *k1, yo, k1, [yo, ssk] 4 times, k9, [k2tog, yo] 4 times, k1, yo; rep from * across, end k3—245 sts.

Row 69: K2, *k1, yo, k1, [yo, ssk] 5 times, k7, [k2tog, yo] 5 times, k1, yo; rep from * across, end k3—261 sts.

Row 71: K2, *k1, yo, k1, [yo, ssk] 6 times, k5, [k2tog, yo] 6 times, k1, yo; rep from * across, end k3—277 sts.

Row 73: K2, *k1, yo, k1, [yo, ssk] 7 times, k3, [k2tog, yo] 7 times, k1, yo; rep from * across, end k3—293 sts.

Row 75: K2, *k1, yo, k1, [yo, ssk] 8 times, k1, [k2tog, yo] 8 times, k1, yo; rep from * across, end k3—309 sts.

Row 77: K2, *k1, yo, k1, [yo, ssk] 8 times, yo, s2kp, yo, [k2tog, yo] 8 times, k1, yo; rep from * across, end k3—325 sts. BO loosely purlwise on WS.

FINISHING

Weave in ends. Block.

Elegant
Cashmere Triangle

material and tools

Artyarns Cashmere 1 (100% cashmere; 1.8 oz/50g = 510yd/466m): (A), 1 skein, color tonal deep green #2261; (B), 1 skein, color tonal olive #2242—approx.1020yds/932m of lace-weight yarn; (🔵)

Knitting Needles: 2.25mm (size 1 U.S.) 32"/81cm circular needle or size to obtain gauge

Crochet hook: 0.60mm (US 16) crochet hook, or size to fit through beads

15g 11/0 bronze Iris seed beads

4 stitch markers

Tapestry needle

gauge

22 sts/28 rows = 4"/10cm In Stockinette Stitch, after blocking

Always take time to check your gauge.

special abbreviations

PB (place bead): Work st as indicated, lift st with crochet hook, slide bead onto st, replace st on right needle

NOTES: *Shawl is worked from the neck down. Slip all markers as you come to them. When changing colors every row, carry unused yarn along edge, twisting it around working yarn to prevent long loops.*

finished measurements

54" wide x 27" deep/137cm x 69cm, after blocking

Create three chevron bands that flow into one another In this versatile piece—wear it as a shawl or a scarf. Tiny beads and simple eyelets, along with an open border, combine for a classic look, allowing the beauty of the yarn to shine through.

design by
Andrea Jurgrau

skill level
experienced

instructions

SEQUENCE 1

With A, CO 3 sts using a provisional method. Knit 8 rows.

Pick up and p 3 sts along one long side of piece.

Undo provisional CO, pick up and k 3 sts—9 sts. Turn.

Row 1 (first sequence only) (RS): K3, PM, yo, k1, yo, PM, k1 (center st), PM, yo, k1, yo, PM, k3—13 sts.

Row 2 and all even rows unless otherwise noted: K3, p to last 3 sts, k3.

Rows 3-19 (odd rows for the first sequence and Rows 1-19 odd rows for subsequent sequences): K3, yo, k to marker, yo, k1 (center st), yo, k to last marker, yo, k3—4 sts inc each row.

Row 21: K3, yo, [k2tog, PB, yo] to 1 st before marker, k1, PB, yo, k1 (center st), yo, k1, PB, [yo, k2tog, PB] to marker, yo, k3.

Rows 23-41 (odd rows): K3, yo, k to marker, yo, k1 (center st), yo, k to marker, yo, k3.

Row 43: With B, k3, yo, k to marker, yo, k1 (center st), yo, k to marker, yo, k3.

Row 44 (RS): Slide work to where color A is attached and with A, k across.

Row 45 (WS): Slide work to where color B is attached and with B, k3, yo, p to marker, yo, p1 (center st), yo, p to marker, yo, k3.

Row 46 (WS): Slide work to where color A is attached and with A, k3, p to last 3 sts, k3.

NOTE: *Work sts for Rows 43-46 as they present themselves, being careful not to twist sts.*

Rep Rows 43-46 a total of 5 times. With B, rep row 21.

Rep Rows 44-46 (following color sequence A, B, A) once.

Rep Rows 43-46 (following color sequence B, A, B, A) a total of 4 times and then rep Rows 43 (with B) and 44 (with A) once.

Cut both yarns, leaving 9"/23cm tails. Slide work to far end of needle, ready to knit.

SEQUENCE 2

With B, rep Rows 1-42.

Rep [Row 43 (with A), Row 44 (with B), Row 45 (with A), Row 46 (with B)] a total of 5 times. With A, rep Row 21. Rep Rows 44-46 (following color sequence B, A, B) once. Rep Rows 43-46 (following color sequence A, B, A, B) a total of 4 times and then rep Row 43 (with A) and Row 44 (with B) once more.

Cut both yarns, leaving 9"/23cm tails. Slide work to far end of needle, ready to knit.

SEQUENCE 3

With A, rep Sequence 1, ending with
Row 22.

BORDER

Row 1: With A, k3, yo, [k2tog, yo] to 1 st
before marker, k1, yo, k1 (center st),
yo, k1, [yo, k2tog] to marker, yo, k3.

Row 2: Knit.

Rep Rows 1 and 2 a total of 3 times.

BO loosely as follows: K2, return 2 sts
to left-hand needle, [k2tog, return 1
st to left-hand needle] and continue
across row until all sts are used.

FINISHING

Weave in ends. Block.

A play on triangles and diamonds results in an interesting shape that lies nicely on the shoulders. By creating modular shapes in a continuous manner, you will not need to cut the yarn throughout.

design by
Iris Schreier

skill level
intermediate

Stepping Stones Shawl

materials and tools

Artyarns Cashmere Glitter (100% cashmere with Lurex; 1.8 oz/50g = 170yd/155m): (A), 1 skein, color multi #106; (B), 1 skein, color white #250—approx 340yd/310m of fine-weight yarn; (2)

Knitting needles: 4.5mm (size 7 U.S.) or size to obtain gauge

Tapestry needle

gauge

16 sts/32 rows = 4"/10cm in Garter Stitch

Always take time to check your gauge.

special abbreviations

K1 f&b: Knit in the front and back of the same stitch

Sl 1: Slip 1 knitwise with yarn in back

Turn: Transfer the left needle to the right hand and the right needle to the left hand, bringing the yarn up and over to the back between the tops of the 2 needles

finished measurements

46" wide x 9" deep/117cm x 23cm

pattern stitches

NOTE: *Each pat is worked as a unit; complete all rows before moving to next group of sts in the row.*

BASE TRIANGLE (worked over 13 sts, inc to 26 sts)

K6, k1 f&b, k1, turn; Sl 1, k1 f&b, k2, turn;

Sl 1, k1, k1 f&b, k3, turn; sl 1, k2, k1 f&b, k4, turn;

Sl 1, k3, k1 f&b, k5, turn; sl 1, k4, k1 f&b, k6, turn;

Sl 1, k5, k1 f&b, k7, turn; sl 1, k6, k1 f&b, k8, turn;

Sl 1, k7, k1 f&b, k9, turn; sl 1, k8, k1 f&b, k10, turn;

Sl 1, k9, k1 f&b, k11, turn; sl 1, k10, k1 f&b, k12, turn;

Sl 1, k11, k1 f&b, k12, do not turn.

DIAMOND (worked over 26 sts)

K12, k1 f&b, ssk, turn; sl 1, k1 f&b, ssk, turn;

Sl 1, k1 f&b, k1, ssk, turn; sl 1, k1, k1 f&b, k1, ssk, turn;

Sl 1, k1, k1 f&b, k2, ssk, turn; sl 1, k2, k1 f&b, k2, ssk, turn;

Sl 1, k2, k1 f&b, k3, ssk, turn; sl 1, k3, k1 f&b, k3, ssk, turn;

Sl 1, k3, k1 f&b, k4, ssk, turn; sl 1, k4, k1 f&b, k4, ssk, turn;

Sl 1, k4, k1 f&b, k5, ssk, turn; sl 1, k5, k1 f&b, k5, ssk, turn;

Sl 1, k5, k1 f&b, k6, ssk, turn; sl 1, k6, k1 f&b, k6, ssk, turn;

Sl 1, k6, k1 f&b, k7, ssk, turn; sl 1, k7, k1 f&b, k7, ssk, turn;

Sl 1, k7, k1 f&b, k8, ssk, turn; sl 1, k8, k1 f&b, k8, ssk, turn;

Sl 1, k8, k1 f&b, k9, ssk, turn; sl 1, k9, k1 f&b, k9, ssk, turn;

Sl 1, k9, k1 f&b, k10, ssk, turn; sl 1, k10, k1 f&b, k10, ssk, turn;

Sl 1, k10, k1 f&b, k11, ssk, turn; sl 1, k11, k1 f&b, k11, ssk, do not turn.

instructions

SHAWL

With A, loosely CO 104 sts.

Row 1: Work 8 Base Triangles—208 sts.

Rows 2–4: With A, [k12, k1 f&b, k11, k2tog] 8 times.

Rows 5–6: With B, [k12, k1 f&b, k11, k2tog] 8 times.

Rows 7–8: With A, [k12, k1 f&b, k11, k2tog] 8 times.

Row 9: With B, k13, [work Diamond] 7 times, k1 f&b, k10, k2tog.

Row 10: With B, k26, [k1 f&b, k11, k2tog, k12] 6 times, k1 f&b, k23, k2tog.

Rows 11–12: With A, rep Row 10.

Rows 13–14: With B, rep Row 10.

Row 15: With A, k26 [work Diamond] 6 times, k1 f&b, k23, k2tog.

Row 16: With A, k39, [k1 f&b, k11, k2tog, k12] 5 times, k1 f&b, k30, k2tog.

Rows 17–18: With B, rep Row 16.

Rows 19–20: With A, rep Row 16.

Row 21: With B, rep Row 16.

BO loosely.

FINISHING

Weave in ends. Block.

Waves Stole

materials and tools

Artyarns Silk Pearl (100% silk; 1.8oz/50g = 170yd/155m): (A), 1 skein, color eggplant #2289; (B), 1 skein, color blush #2271—approx 340yds/310m of fine-weight yarn;

Knitting needles: 4.5mm (size 7 U.S.) or size to obtain gauge

Crochet hook: 5.0mm (size H-8 U.S.)

Tapestry needle

gauge

20 sts/20 rows = 4" (10 cm) in Wave Pattern

Always take time to check your gauge.

special technique

Wrap and turn: Work to indicated st, sl next st pwise, move yarn between needles, sl st back to left needle, move yarn back, turn (see Assorted Techniques, page 126)

special abbreviation

Turn: Transfer the left needle to the right hand and the right needle to the left hand, bringing the yarn up and over to the back between the tops of the 2 needles

finished measurements

32" long x 11" deep/81cm x 28cm

The undulating waves of this design enhance the drastic difference between the two colors, making a vibrant contrast. This is a bold way to integrate the different colors.

Design by
Iris Schreier

skill level
experienced
● ● ● ●

pattern stitches

WAVE

[K1, p1] 5 times, wrap and turn; [k1, p1] 4 times, wrap and turn; [k1, p1] 3 times, wrap and turn; [k1, p1] 3 times.

NOTES: *Knit or purl wraps tog with st when indicated.*

Work this pat with a multiple of 18 + 2 sts. Rows 1–2 make up 3 full Waves, while Rows 9–10 make up ½ Wave, followed by 2 full Waves, followed by ½ Wave.

instructions

SHAWL

With A, CO 56 sts.

Row 1 (RS): With A, [k1, p1] 8 times, wrap and turn; *work Wave Pattern, [k1, picking up wrap, p1] twice, [k1, p1] 8 times, wrap and turn; rep from *1 time; work Wave Pattern, [k1, picking up wrap, p1] twice, [k1, p1] 1 time.

Row 2: With A, [k1, p1] across, picking up all wraps.

Rows 3–4: With A, knit.

Rows 5–8: With D, k1, [yo, ssk] to last st, k1.

Row 9: With A, [k1, p1] 3 times, wrap and turn; [k1, p1] 3 times, turn; [k1, p1] twice, wrap and turn; [k1, p1] twice, turn; [k1, p1] twice, [k1, picking up wraps, p1] twice, [k1, p1] 8 times, wrap and turn; work Wave Pattern, [k1, picking up wrap, p1] twice, [k1, p1] 8 times, wrap and turn; work Wave Pattern, [k1, picking up wrap, p1] twice, [k1, p1] 8 times, turn; [k1, p1] 3 times, wrap and turn; [k1, p1] 3 times, turn; [k1, p1] twice, wrap and turn, [k1, p1] twice.

Row 10: With A, *k1, p1; rep from * across, picking up all wraps.

Rows 11–12: With A, knit.

Rows 13–16: Rep Rows 5–8.

Rep Rows 1–16 for pat until piece measures 32"/81cm or desired length. With A, BO.

FINISHING

With crochet hook and B, work 1 rnd of single crochet around edges. Fasten off.

Weave in ends. Block.

Diamond Lace Wrap

materials and tools

Artyarns Ensemble (75% silk, 25% cashmere; 3.5oz/100gr = 256yd/234m): (A), 1 skein, color greens #H2; (B), 1 skein, color tonal blue #2204—approx 512yds/468m of medium-weight yarn;

Knitting needles: 5.0mm (size 8 U.S.) or size to obtain gauge

Tapestry needle

gauge

10 sts/14 rows = 4"/10cm in Diamond Pattern

Always take time to check your gauge.

finished measurements

68" wide x 23" deep/173cm x 58cm

Use short rows and lace in a very unusual manner to construct a shawl consisting of exquisite diamonds. The wrap resembles a triangle with enough length to wrap around you quite comfortably.

design by
Iris Schreier

skill level
intermediate

pattern stitches

NOTE: Each pat is worked as a unit; complete all rows before moving to next group of sts in the row.

RIGHT SIDE DIAMOND
(inc from 2 to 11 sts)

With new color, using knitted cast on, CO 2 sts, twist yarns.

K1, yo, k1, yo, ssk, turn; sl 1, p4, twist yarns to carry up unused yarn;

K2, yo, k1, yo, k1, ssk, turn; sl 1, p6, twist yarns to carry up unused yarn;

K3, yo, k1, yo, k2, ssk, turn; sl 1, p8, twist yarns to carry up unused yarn;

K4, yo, k1, yo, k3, ssk, turn; sl 1, p10, twist yarns to carry up unused yarn;

K1, ssk, k2, yo, k1, yo, k2, k2tog, k1.

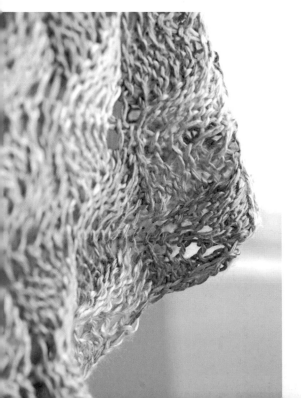

LEFT SIDE DIAMOND
(inc from 4 to 11 sts)

K5 (end of row). Using knitted cast on, CO 4 sts.

P4, p2tog, turn; sl 1, k1, yo, k1, yo, k2;

P6, p2tog, turn; sl 1, k2, yo, k1, yo, k3;

P8, p2tog, turn; sl 1, k3, yo, k1, yo, k4;

P10, p2tog, turn; sl 1, ssk, k2, yo, k1, yo, k2, k2tog, k1.

DIAMOND
(worked over 11 sts)

K5, yo, k1, yo, ssk, turn; sl 1, p3, p2tog, turn;

Sl 1, k1, yo, k1, yo, k1, ssk, turn; sl 1, p5, p2tog, turn;

Sl 1, k2, yo, k1, yo, k2, ssk, turn; sl 1, p7, p2tog, turn;

Sl 1, k3, yo, k1, yo, k3, ssk, turn; sl 1, p9, p2tog, turn;

Sl 1, ssk, k2, yo, k1, yo, k2, k2tog, k1, do not turn.

instructions

SHAWL

With A, CO 35 sts.

Row 1: With A, [work Diamond, k1] twice, work Diamond.

Row 2: With A, purl.

Row 3: With B, work Right Side Diamond, k1, [work Diamond, k1] 2 times, work Left Side Diamond.

Row 4: With B, purl.

Row 5: With A, work Right Side Diamond, k1, [work Diamond, k1] 3 times, work Left Side Diamond.

Row 6: With A, purl.

Row 7: With B, work Right Side Diamond, k1, [work Diamond, k1] 4 times, work Left Side Diamond.

Row 8: With B, purl.

Rows 9–28: Rep rows 7–8, alternating 2 rows A and 2 rows B and adding one more [Diamond, k1] rep to each new row to reach edge before working Left Side Diamond.

Row 29: With A, work Right Side Diamond, k1, [work Diamond, k1] 15 times, work Left Side Diamond—203 sts. BO loosely.

FINISHING

Weave in ends. Block.

This clever lace wrap is designed to drape gracefully around your shoulders and be held in place by slipping one end through a channel at the opposite end. For added sparkle, one of the yarns is occasionally worked double-stranded in the lace pattern.

design by
Lynn M. Wilson

skill level
intermediate

Smart Shawl

materials and tools

Artyarns Mohair Splash (74% silk, 26% mohair with glass beads and sequins; 1.8oz/50g = 165yd/151m): (A), 1 skein, color gold #223 —approx 165yd/151m of lightweight yarn; ③

Artyarns Silk Rhapsody Glitter (80% silk, 20% mohair with metallic; 3.5oz/100g = 260yd/238m): (B), 1 skein, color goldenrod #H12 —approx 260yd/238m of medium-weight yarn; ④

Knitting needles: 5.0mm (size 8 U.S.) 24"/61cm circular needle; 5.0mm (size 8 U.S.) straight; 6mm (size 10 U.S.) straight; 8mm (size 11 U.S.) needles or size to obtain gauge

Waste yarn

Tapestry needle

gauge

13 sts/13 rows = 4"/10cm in Lace Pattern using largest needles and B, after blocking

Always take time to check your gauge.

finished measurements

Approx 62" wide x 13" deep/157cm x 33cm, after blocking

instructions

CHANNEL

With smallest needles and A, using a
provisional method, CO 43 sts.

Row 1 (RS): Knit.

Row 2: Purl.

Row 3: Sl 1, k3, *yo, k3, pass first st of
k3 over other 2 sts; rep from * to last
3 sts, k3.

Rows 4, 6, 8: Sl 1, purl to last 2 sts, k2.

Row 5: Sl 1, k2, *yo, k3, pass first st of
k3 over other 2 sts; rep from * to last
4 sts, k1.

Row 7: Sl 1, *yo, k3, pass first st of k3
over other 2 sts; rep from * to last 2
sts, k2.

Rep Rows 3–8 six times more. Remove
provisional CO and place sts on
circular 5.0mm needle. Fold in half
with RS facing; knit each st tog with
corresponding st from CO row —
43 sts.

Next row (WS): Sl 1, k1, p to last 2 sts,
k2.

WRAP SECTION

Change to medium-size needles
and B.

Row 1 (RS): Sl 1, k to end.

Row 2: Sl 1, k1, *k1, yo, k2tog; rep from *
to last 2 sts, k2.

Rows 3–4: Rep Rows 1 and 2.

Change to largest needles and rep
Row 2 twelve times more, ending
with a WS row. *Change to a double
strand of A and rep Row 2 twice.
Change to B and rep Row 2 eigh-
teen times. Rep from * 7 times
more. **With double strand of A,
rep Row 2 twice. Change to B and
rep Row 2 twice. Rep from ** until
piece measures approx 61"/155cm.
Change to double strand of A and
rep Row 2 twice.

Next Row: Sl 1, k2, *k1 tbl, k2; rep from *
to last st, k1. BO.

FINISHING

Weave in ends. Block.

Mesh Wrap

Here is a sparkling wrap that is spectacular over evening wear—perfect over the little black dress that needs a little extra coverage. It has enough pizzazz for any special occasion!

design by
Iris Schreier

skill level
easy

materials and tools

Artyarns Beaded Pearl & Sequins (100% silk with glass beads and sequins; 1.8oz/50g = 80yd/73m): (A), 1 skein, color tonal black with silver beads and sequins #2246S—approx 80yd/73m of medium-weight yarn; (4)

Artyarns Silk Pearl (100% silk; 1.8oz/50g = 170yd/155m): (B), 1 skein, color tonal black #2246—approx 170yd/155m of lightweight yarn; (3)

Knitting needles: 10.0mm (size 15 U.S.) 29"/74cm circular needle or size to obtain gauge

Tapestry needle

gauge

9 sts/16 rows = 4"/10cm in Pattern

Always take time to check your gauge.

finished measurements

66" wide x 20" deep/168cm x 51cm

instructions

WRAP

With A, CO 3 sts. Alternate 2 rows A and 4 rows B throughout.

Row 1: Knit in the front, back, and front of the same st, knit to end— 2 sts inc.

Rep Row 1 until there are 149 sts. BO loosely.

FINISHING

Weave in ends. Block.

Asymmetric Shawlette

materials and tools

Artyarns Silk Rhapsody Glitter Gold (80% silk, 20% mohair with metallic; 3.5oz/100g = 260yds/238m): (A), 1 skein, color gray #247—approx 260yds/238m of medium-weight yarn;

Artyarns Ensemble (75% silk, 25% cashmere; 3.5oz/100g = 256yds/234m): (B), 1 skein, color gray #247—approx 256yds/234m of medium-weight yarn;

Knitting needles: 9mm (size 13 U.S.) or size to obtain gauge

Crochet hook: 8mm (size L-11 U.S.)—optional

Tapestry needle

gauge

8 sts/14 rows = 4"/10cm in Lace Pattern using A and B held tog

Always take time to check your gauge.

special abbreviations for optional crochet trim

Sc: Single crochet

Ch: Chain

Dc: Double crochet

finished measurements

44" long x 14" wide/112cm x 36cm

This shawlette is quick to knit, and the combination of two beautiful yarns adds luxury and depth. Worked in a simple lace pattern that adds fluidity and sophistication, this piece is a great addition to any wardrobe.

design by
Tanya Alpert

skill level
beginner
● ● ● ●

pattern stitch

LACE (multiple of 4 + 2 sts):
Row 1 (RS): K2, *yo, k2tog, k2; rep from
* across.

Row 2: K2, purl to last 2 sts, k2.

Row 3: K2, *k2tog, yo, k2; rep from *
across.

Row 4: Rep row 2.

Rep rows 1–4 for pat.

instructions

SHAWLETTE

With A and B held tog, CO 34 sts.

Row 1 (RS): Knit.

Row 2: K2, p to last 2 sts, k2. Change
to Lace Pattern and work even until
piece measures 44"/112cm from
beg. BO loosely.

FINISHING

With WS facing, sew BO edge to the
side edge, 6"/15cm down from CO
edge, letting seam show on RS.

CROCHET TRIM (optional):

Row 1: With crochet hook and A and B held tog, sc, *ch 3, sc; rep from * across seam, turn.

Row 2: Ch 6 (counts as first dc and ch 3), dc in sc, ch 5, *(dc, ch 3, dc) in sc, ch 5; rep from * across, end (dc, ch 3, dc) in last sc, turn.

Row 3: Ch 3, sc in ch-3 space, ch 3, *(dc, ch 3, dc) into ch-5 space, ch 3, sc into ch-3 space, ch 3; rep from * across. Fasten off. Weave in ends. Block.

Stacking Shells Shawl

Here is lace at its best in this breathtaking shawl with a beautiful pattern. The beaded trimming adds a little glamour; it's so soft and light that you will never want to take it off.

design by
Daniela Johannsenova

skill level
intermediate

materials and tools

Artyarns Silk Mohair (60% mohair, 40% silk; 0.9oz/25g = 312yd/285m): (A), 1 skein, color fleshtone #H10—approx 312yd/285m of lace-weight yarn; (0)

Artyarns Beaded Mohair & Sequins (80% silk with glass beads and sequins; 1.8oz/50g = 114yd/104m): (B), 1 skein, color fleshtone #H10—approx 114yd/104m of lightweight yarn; (3)

Knitting needles: 5.0mm (size 8 U.S.) 32"/81cm circular needle or size to obtain gauge

Crochet hook: 5.0mm (size H-8 U.S.)

Stitch markers

Tapestry needle

gauge

16 sts/32 rows = 4"/10cm in Garter Stitch

Always take time to check your gauge.

special abbreviation

Yo2: Wrap yarn over needle 2 times as though to create 2 sts

finished measurements

46" wide x 22" deep/117cm x 56cm

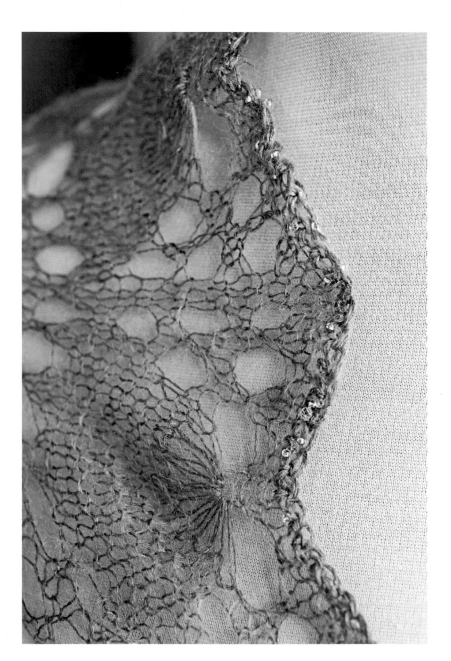

pattern stitches

LOXI
(multiple of 19 sts; st count changes from row to row)

Row 1 (WS): Knit.

Row 2: Knit.

Row 3: *K1, yo2, p2tog tbl, k13, p2tog, yo2, k1; rep from * across.

Row 4: *K2, p1, k15, p1, k2; rep from * across.

Rows 5–6: Knit.

Row 7: *K1, (yo2, p2tog tbl) twice, k11, (p2tog, yo2) twice, k1; rep from * across.

Row 8: *K2, p1, k1, p1, k14, [p1, k2] twice; rep from * across.

Row 9: Knit.

Row 10: *K6, (yo2, k1) 14 times, k5; rep from * across.

Row 11: *K1, (yo2, p2tog tbl) twice, yo2, sl next 15 sts, dropping yo's (creating 15 elongated sts), p these 15 sts tog, (yo2, p2tog) twice, yo2, k1; rep from * across.

Row 12: *K1, p1, [k2, p1] twice, k3, [p1, k2] twice, p1, k1; rep from * across.

Rep Rows 1–12 for pat.

NOTE: PM between each rep of pat.

instructions

SHAWL

CO 21 sts.

Row 1 (WS): K1, work Row 1 of Loxi pat to last st, k1.

Row 2: K1, work row 2 of Loxi pat to last st, k1. Cont as set for a total of 24 rows.

Note: Beg and end each row with k1 throughout.

Next 2 rows: CO 19 sts at beg of next 2 rows, knitting across. Rep Loxi pat 3 times across, twice (total of 24 rows)—59 sts. Next 2 rows: CO 19 sts at beg of next 2 rows, knitting across. Rep Loxi pat 5 times across, twice (total of 24 rows)—97 sts.

Next 2 rows: CO 19 sts at beg of next 2 rows, knitting across. Rep Loxi pat 7 times across, twice (total of 24 rows)—135 sts.

Next 2 rows: CO 19 sts at beg of next 2 rows, knitting across. Rep Loxi pat 9 times across, twice (total of 24 rows)—173 sts. BO loosely.

FINISHING

With crochet hook and B, work 1 rnd of single crochet around edges. Fasten off. Weave in ends. Block.

Striped Möbius

materials and tools

Artyarns Silk Rhapsody Glitter (50% silk with Lurex, 50% kid mohair; 3.5oz/100g = 260yd/238m): (A), 1 skein, color gold tones with gold metallic #118G, (B), 1 skein, color gold with gold metallic #1009— approx 520yds/476m of medium-weight yarn;

Knitting needles: 5.0mm (size 8 U.S.) 36"/91cm circular needle or size to obtain gauge

Stitch markers

Tapestry needle

gauge

16 sts/24 rows = 4"/10cm in K3, P3 Rib

Always take time to check your gauge

special technique

Möbius Cast On (see page 124)

finished measurements

34" circumference x 12" deep/86cm x 30cm

Wear this over the shoulders as a wrap, or around the neck as a warm cowl—no matter what you do with it, it will stay in place. The secret is the Möbius twist that builds this piece from the center out.

design by
Iris Schreier

skill level
intermediate

instructions

MÖBIUS

With A, CO 144 sts using Möbius Cast On—288 sts total. PM.

Rounds 1-2: With A, *k3, p3; rep from * around.

Rounds 3-5: With B, *k3, p3; rep from * around.

Rounds 6-8: With A, *k3, p3; rep from * around.

Rounds 9-26: Rep Rnds 3–8.

Rounds 27-30: *K1, p1; rep from * around. BO loosely.

FINISHING

Weave in ends. Block.

Bridal Shrug

materials and tools

Artyarns Beaded Mohair & Sequins (80% silk, 20% kid mohair; 1.8oz/50g = 104yd/95m): (A), 1 skein, color white with silver sequins and beads #250—approx 104yd/95m of lightweight yarn;

Artyarns Silk Mohair (60% kid mohair, 40% silk; 0.9oz/25g = 312yd/285m): (B), 1 skein, color white #250—approx 312yd/285m of lace-weight yarn;

Knitting needles: 4.5mm (size 7 U.S.) and 6mm (size 10 U.S.) needles or size to obtain gauge

Stitch marker

Tapestry needle

gauge

16 sts/22 rows= 4"/10cm in Lace Pattern using smaller needles

Always take time to check your gauge.

special abbreviation

K3tog: Knit 3 sts together as though they were 1st, a decrease of 2 sts

finished measurements

Across Back: 21 (25, 29)"/53 (64, 74)cm

Length: 13"/33cm

Enhance the wedding or party experience with a sparkling shrug, providing warmth, elegance, and delight.

design by
Iris Schreier

skill level
intermediate

instructions

SHRUG

With smaller needles and A, CO 42 sts.

Rows 1-2: With A, knit.

Row 3 (RS): With B, k1, *yo, k2tog, yo, ssk; rep from * to last st, k1.

Rows 4-6: With B, knit. Carry unused yarn along edge, twisting it around working yarn to prevent long loops. Rep Rows 1-6 until piece measures 47"/119cm. BO.

FINISHING

With WS facing, fold lengthwise and sew a 10 (8, 6)"/25 (20, 15)cm seam in from each end for sleeves.

TRIM

With larger needles and B, pick up 1 st in each row around opening. PM and join.

Round 1: [K1, yo, k1] into each st around.

Round 2: Knit.

Round 3: [K3tog, leaving sts on left needle, yo, k3tog again, then transfer from left to right needle] around, maintaining st count. BO loosely.

Weave in ends. Block.

Cashmere Bolero

materials and tools

Artyarns Cashmere 2 (100% 2-strand cashmere; 1.8oz/50g = 225yd/233m): (A), 1 skein, color crème d'orange #137—approx 225yd/233m of super fine-weight yarn;

Artyarns Beaded Cashmere & Sequins (65% silk with glass beads and sequins, 35% cashmere; 1.8oz/50g = 90yd/82m): (B), 1 skein, color gold #259—approx 90yd/82m of medium-weight yarn;

Knitting needles: 4.5mm (size 7 U.S.) straight; 32"/81cm circular; and set of 5 dpns or size to obtain gauge

Stitch marker

Tapestry needle

gauge

20 sts/24 rows=4"/10cm in Stockinette Stitch

Always take time to check your gauge.

special abbreviation

S2kp: Slip 2, knit 1, pass slipped stitches over

finished measurements

31" wide x 12" deep/79cm x 30cm

This is a great little piece that can be worn with jeans or something far more sophisticated. The beads and sequins add fun to the shrug.

design by
Sharon Sorken

skill level
intermediate
● ● ● ●

pattern stitch

LACE (multiple of 10 + 15 sts):

Row 1: K2, k2tog, *k3, yo, k1, yo, k3, s2kp; rep from * to last 11 sts, k3, yo, k1, yo, k3, ssk, k2.

Row 2 and all even rows through 16: K2, purl to last 2 sts, k2.

Row 3: K2, k2tog,*k2, yo, k3, yo, k2, s2kp; rep from * to last 11 sts, k2, yo, k3, yo, k2, ssk, k2.

Row 5: K2, k2tog, *k1, yo, k5, yo, k1, s2kp; rep from * to last 11 sts, k1, yo, k5, yo, k1, ssk, k2.

Row 7: K2, k2tog, *yo, k7, yo, s2kp; rep from * to last 11 sts, yo, k7, yo, ssk, k2.

Row 9: K3, *yo, k3, s2kp, k3, yo, k1; rep from * to last 12 sts, yo, k3, s2kp, k3, yo, k3.

Row 11: K3, *k1, yo, k2, s2kp, k2, yo, k2; rep from * to last 12 sts, k1, yo, k2, s2kp, k2, yo, k4.

Row 13: K3, *k2, yo, k1, s2kp, k1, yo, k3; rep from * to last 12 sts, k2, yo, k1, s2kp,k1, yo, k5.

Row 15: K3, *k3, yo, s2kp, yo, k4; rep from * to last 12 sts, k3, yo, s2kp, yo, k6.

Rep Rows 1–16 for pat.

pattern chart

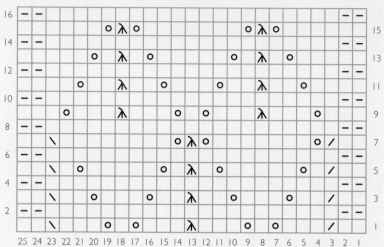

λ		sk2 p
/		k2 tog
\		ssk
☐		knit on RS, purl on WS
−		purl on WS, knit on RS
o		yo

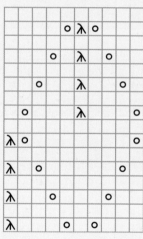

instructions

SHRUG

Wind off approximately 4 yds/4m of A for assembly and set aside.

With straight needles and A, CO 45 sts. Work in Lace Pattern until almost all yarn is used. BO.

FINISHING

Holding the piece lengthwise, mark the center top edge with WS facing.

Fold each end to meet the marker. With A, seam the shoulders.

BORDER

With circular needle and B, RS facing, pick up 192 sts around the body opening. PM and join.

Round 1: *Yo, k1, sk2p, k1, yo, k1; rep from * around.

Round 2: Knit.

Rounds 3–8: Rep Rnds 1–2.

Round 9: *K1, yo; rep from * around. BO loosely.

SLEEVE TRIM

With B and dpns, pick up 36 sts around armhole opening. Work as for Border.

Weave in ends. Block.

Eyelet Collar

Want style and warmth at the same time? Cozy up in this snug turtleneck collar with lacy stripes and a touch of sparkle. The pattern is simple enough to follow whilst snuggled up on the couch with a good movie.

design by
Heather Dixon

skill level
intermediate

materials and tools

Artyarns Silk Rhapsody (50% silk, 50% kid mohair; 3.5oz/100g = 260yds/238m): (A), 1 skein, color teal blue #279—approx 260yds/238m of medium-weight yarn;

Artyarns Beaded Silk Light (100% silk with glass beads; 1.8oz/50g = 160yds/146m): (B), 1 skein, color multi #1009G—approx 100yds/91m of lightweight yarn;

Knitting needles: 3.75mm (size 5 U.S.) 16"/41cm circular needle (or set of 5 dpns) or size to obtain gauge

4.5mm (size 7 U.S.) needles

Stitch marker

Yarn needle

gauge

20 sts/36 rows = 4"/10cm in K2, P2 Rib Pattern using smaller needles and A

Always take time to check your gauge.

finished measurements

16"/41cm neck circumference

instructions

COLLAR

With larger needles and A, CO 80 sts. PM and join, being careful not to twist. Change to smaller needles.

Rounds 1–39: *K2, p2; rep from * around.

Round 40: *K2, p2; rep from * around, remove marker, k1. Change to larger needles and B. Beg working back and forth in rows.

Row 1 (RS): With B, knit.

Row 2: K1, p to last st, k1. Change to A.

Rows 3–4: Knit. Change to B.

Rows 5–6: Knit.

Row 7: K2, *yo, k2tog; rep from * to last 2 sts, k2.

Row 8: Knit. Change to A.

Row 9: Knit.

Row 10: K1, p to last st, k1.

Row 11: Knit.

Row 12: K1, p to last st, k1. Change to B.

Rows 13–14: Knit. Change to A.

Row 15: Knit.

Row 16: K1, p to last st, k1. Change to B.

Rows 17–18: Knit.

Row 19: K2, *yo, k2tog; rep from * to last 2 sts, k2

Row 20: K1, p to last st, k1.

Row 21: K2, *k2tog, yo; rep from * to last 2 sts, k2.

Row 22: K1, p to last st, k1.

Row 23: K2, *yo, k2tog; rep from * to last 2 sts, k2

Row 24: Knit. Change to A

Rows 25–30: Knit.

Rep rows 1–30 once more. Change to B.

Knit 1 row. BO loosely.

FINISHING

Weave in ends. Block.

The perfect accessory for a little sleeveless dress, this shrug is comfortable and elegant. The exquisite sequins and beads give it just enough glimmer without being too flashy, and the alternated silk mohair creates light, airy stitches.

design by
Iris Schreier

skill level
intermediate

Peekaboo Shrug

materials and tools

Artyarns Beaded Rhapsody & Sequins (85% silk with glass beads and sequins, 15% kid mohair with metallic; 3.5oz/100g = 128yd/117m): (A), 1 skein, color gold/tonal black with gold beads and sequins #2246— approx 120yd/110m of medium-weight yarn; (4)

Artyarns Silk Mohair (60% kid mohair, 40% silk; 0.9oz/25g = 312yd/285m): (B), 1 skein, color tonal black #2246—approx 312yd/285m of lace-weight yarn; (0)

Knitting needles: 5.5mm (size 9 U.S.) needles or size to obtain gauge

Stitch markers

Tapestry needle

gauge

14 sts/14 rows = 4"/10cm in Pattern Stitch

Always take time to check your gauge.

special abbreviation

S2kp: Slip 2, knit 1, pass slipped stitches over

finished measurements

40" long x 10" wide/102cm x 25cm

instructions

SHRUG

With A, CO 35 sts. Alternate 2 rows of
   A and 2 rows of B throughout.

Row 1 (RS): K1, *yo, s2kp, yo, k3; rep
   from * to last 4 sts, yo, s2kp, yo, k1.

Row 2: Knit.

Rep Rows 1 and 2 until piece measures approx 40"/102cm or desired
   length, ending with Row 1 in A. BO.

FINISHING

Fold in half lengthwise. With B, seam
   11"/28cm in from each end to form
   sleeves. Weave in ends. Block.

techniques

Here are the commonly used techniques in *One + One: Scarves, Shawls & Shrugs*.

Casting On

Most of the projects in this book use the long-tail cast on described below; assume you are to cast on using this method unless otherwise specified. Some of the projects use alternate cast-on techniques that also are detailed in this section.

LONG-TAIL CAST-ON

Leaving a tail long enough to cast on the required number of stitches (1 inch per stitch is plenty), make a slipknot, and place it on the needle. *Wrap the tail around your thumb and the working yarn around your index finger. Hold the yarn ends with your other three fingers (*figure 1*). Insert the needle into the loop around your thumb from front to back and over the yarn around your index finger (*figures 2 and 3*). Bring the needle down through the loop on your thumb (*figure 4*). Drop the loop off your thumb and tighten the stitch. Repeat from * for the required number of stitches.

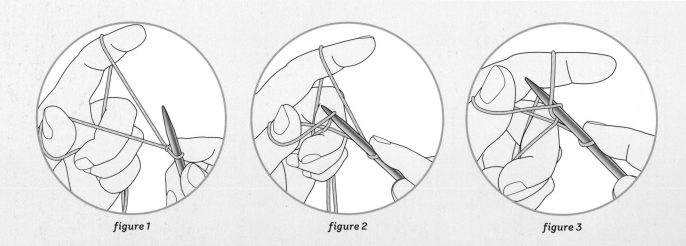

figure 1   *figure 2*   *figure 3*

KNITTED-ON CAST-ON

This method can be used to begin a project, and it also allows you to add new stitches to stitches you've already knitted. If you don't have stitches on your needle yet, cast on one stitch by placing a slipknot on the needle, and hold the needle in your left hand.

Insert the right needle into the first stitch on the left needle, as if to knit it. Knit the stitch, but don't drop the stitch from the left needle. Place the newly knitted stitch back on the left needle (*figure 5*). Continue adding new stitches in this manner until you have added as many stitches as the pattern calls for.

PROVISIONAL CAST-ON

A provisional cast-on allows you to knit from both the top and bottom of each cast-on stitch. Once you've knitted a few rows, the stitches can be put back on needles and knitted in the other direction. A smooth, contrasting color of scrap yarn can easily be identified and undone to expose the live stitches.

Using a crochet hook and smooth scrap yarn, chain the number of stitches called for in the pattern, plus an additional five or so. On one side of the chain, the stitches form Vs, and on the other side of the chain, the stitches form bumps. Insert the knitting needle into the bump of the stitch next to the one forming the loop on the hook and knit it (*figure 6*). Continue along the chain, knitting into each following bump, until you have the number of stitches required by the pattern. Now attach the main knitting yarn and start to knit as instructed. After several rows of knitting, or when directed in the pattern, remove the scrap yarn and carefully transfer the live stitches at the bottom edge to a knitting needle. You'll now be able to work these stitches in the other direction.

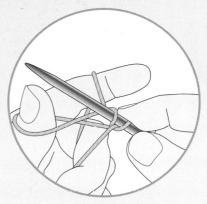

figure 4

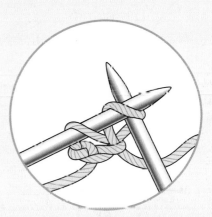

figure 5

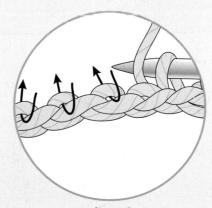

figure 6

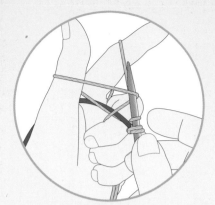

figure 7

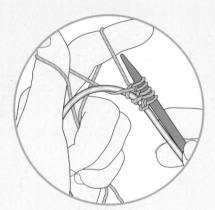

figure 8

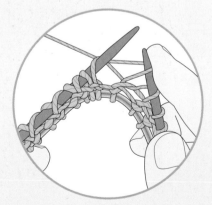

figure 9

MÖBIUS CAST-ON

A Möbius is a never-ending twisted loop that is created when a circular needle is used with the cable coiled. Use the long-tail cast-on method to attach stitches to the top and bottom of your piece at the same time. Every stitch that you cast on will actually result in a double stitch—the top of the stitch will be on the needle, and the bottom of the stitch will be on the coil.

Use an extra-long circular needle (a minimum of 36 inches/91cm). Wrap the cable into a coil and hold the right needle tip and cable in your right hand. Leaving a long tail for casting on, make a slipknot and place it on the needle so that the tail and the working yarn are in front of the cable. With your left hand, reach under the cable from behind and pick up the tail and the working yarn, holding them in position for the long-tail cast-on. With your thumb in front of the cable, your index finger behind the cable, and the cable resting between your thumb and index finger, cast on the first stitch (*figure 7*). To cast on the next stitch, bring your thumb and the loop of yarn through the coil to the back of the cable (*figure 8*).

Continue casting on by alternately placing your thumb under and in front of the cable, then under and behind the cable, until you have the number of stitches specified in the pattern. When you're ready to knit the first round, place a marker to identify the start of the round, as in ordinary circular knitting. On the first half of the stitches, every other stitch will appear as a twisted stitch—one stitch will lean away from the tip of the needle and the stitch following it will lean toward the tip of the needle. Knit (or purl) the stitches leaning away from the tip of the needle through the front of the stitch, as usual, but knit (or purl) the stitches leaning toward the tip of the needle through the back of the stitch to untwist them. Figure 9 shows how to knit through the back part of the stitch when the stitch is leaning toward the tip of the needle. Note that the next stitch is leaning away from the tip of the needle, and therefore it will be knitted in the regular manner. The remaining half of the stitches will appear as ordinary stitches, so knit (or purl) those as usual, through the front part of the stitch.

Picking Up Stitches

Some projects require that stitches be picked up from the bound-off (horizontal) or side (vertical) edge of a knitted piece. Work with the right side facing you. On the horizontal edge, insert the needle into the first stitch under the bound-off edge and pull a loop through; on the vertical edge, insert the needle between the running threads of the first two stitches and pull a loop through. Continue in this fashion as directed in the pattern.

Binding Off

There are many ways to bind off; here are several techniques used in the book.

LOOSE CAST-OFF

The easiest way to cast off loosely is by using larger needles. If these are not available, merely knit every other stitch twice before binding it off. Work as follows: *Knit one stitch. Knit a second stitch. Transfer the last stitch knitted back to the left-hand needle; knit it again. Bind it off by pulling the first stitch on the right-hand needle over it; repeat from *.

CROCHET BIND-OFF

This is another method of loosely binding off. Insert a crochet hook through the first stitch to be cast off as if you were knitting it, catch the yarn on the hook, draw it through the stitch on the needle, and drop the original stitch from needle. The first stitch is now on the crochet hook. Continue working as follows: *Insert the hook into the next stitch on the needle knitwise, catch the yarn on the hook, and draw it through the stitch on the needle and the stitch on the hook in one continuous motion. The first stitch is now bound off and the second stitch is on the hook; drop it from the needle. Repeat from * across until all the stitches are bound off. Cut the yarn and fasten off the last stitch on the crochet hook (figure 10).

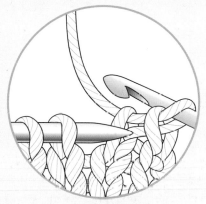

figure 10

THREE-NEEDLE BIND-OFF

The three-needle bind-off is used to join two pieces together while binding off, eliminating the need to sew seams. With the right sides of the knitted fabric that you're joining facing each other, hold the two needles together in your left hand. With a third needle in your right hand, knit two stitches together, working one stitch from the front needle and one stitch from the back needle. *Knit the next two stitches together as before, taking one stitch from the front and one from the back. Pass the previous stitch worked over the latest stitch worked, to bind off. Repeat from * until all stitches have been bound off (figure 11).

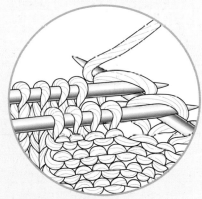

figure 11

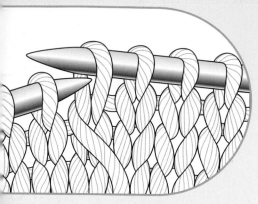

figure 12

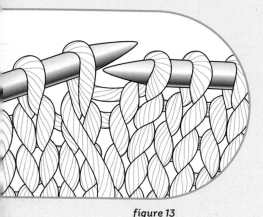

figure 13

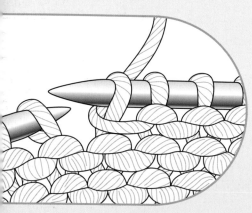

figure 14

Assorted Techniques

A few miscellaneous techniques are used in some of the projects in *One + One: Scarves, Shawls & Shrugs.*

CARRYING YARNS

Here are two scenarios:
When one yarn is used for two rows, it is fairly simple to carry one yarn up along the side when working with the other. Not much thought needs to be given when the yarns alternate every other row.

When yarn is carried along for more than two rows, as in the Taj Mahal Scarf (page 32), you will need to fasten the unworked yarn every two rows by twisting it from behind and around to the front of the working yarn. Otherwise the loopy edge will be unattractive and detract from the garment. Make sure not to pull too tightly or leave the yarn too loose. You will need to maintain good tension so that the piece will lie properly.

SHORT ROWS WITH AND WITHOUT WRAPS

Diagonal short rows with decrease joins do not require wraps, so little need be said except that it is important to follow the instructions exactly and never stop to take a break in the middle of a row. Always break only after you have knitted back and all your stitches are on one needle. The Diamond Spiral (page 48), the Stepping Stones Shawl (page 78), and the Diamond Lace Wrap (page 86) are made with this type of short-row construction.

However, the Waves Stole (page 82) and the Crown Royale Crescent (page 28) use short rows that are knitted in a standard fashion. You will find that the instructions tell you to wrap and turn the short rows. Wrap short rows as follows:

If knitting in the pattern, when instructions say "wrap and turn," slip the next stitch purlwise, bring the yarn forward between the needles from the back to the front, slip the same stitch back to the left needle, take the yarn back between the needles, and turn the work to purl back (*figures 12 and 13*).

If purling in the pattern, when the instructions say "wrap and turn," slip the next stitch purlwise, take the yarn between the needles from the front to the back, slip the same stitch back to the left needle, bring the yarn back between the needles, and turn the work to knit back (figures 14 and 15).

When all the short rows are worked, smooth the transition between the extra rows and close up the holes from the turns by picking up the wrap along with its stitch on the return row. The technique is slightly different for knit and purl stitches.

If a knit stitch:

Knit to the wrapped stitch. Insert the needle knitwise into the wrap and the stitch that was wrapped; knit them together, dropping the wrap to the purl side of the work (figure 16).

If a purl stitch:

Purl to the wrapped stitch. Insert the right-hand needle into the back loop of the wrap and place it on the left-hand needle. Purl the wrap along with the stitch that was wrapped (figure 17).

ADDING BEADS AS YOU KNIT

The Elegant Cashmere Triangle (page 74) features an easy technique for adding beads to your knitting. Put a bead on a crochet hook that's thin enough to accommodate it; use the hook to slip the left stitch off the needle. Slide the bead over the end of the hook and onto the stitch. Replace the beaded stitch on the left needle without twisting it. Now knit the beaded stitch.

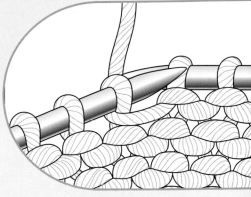

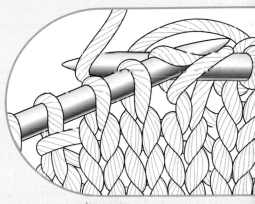

figure 15

figure 16

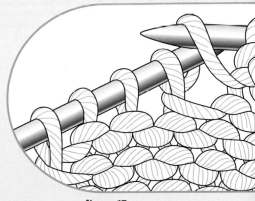

figure 17

figure 18

figure 19

Finishing Details and Decorative Elements

Here are a few last techniques to finish your projects successfully.

MATTRESS STITCH

A mattress stitch joins two pieces of stockinette in such a way that the knitting appears to be continuous. Use a darning needle threaded with the same yarn used in the project, block the two pieces you are seaming, and hold them side by side with the right sides facing you. Insert the needle under the horizontal bar between the edge stitch and the one next to it, pulling the yarn through the bar, and insert the needle under the matching bar on the opposing piece. Continue in this fashion until you have completed the seam (*figure 18*).

I-CORDS

An I-cord is formed with a special three-pronged gadget, or by simply knitting a few stitches in the round with two double-pointed needles as follows:

Cast three stitches onto one double-pointed needle; do not turn. *Slide the stitches to the opposite end of the needle and hold it in your left hand, with the right side of the work facing you. Draw the working yarn to the right behind the cast-on stitches, and using the second double-pointed needle, knit the three stitches again. Repeat from * until the I-cord is the desired length. As you work, be sure to draw the working yarn somewhat tightly across the back of the stitches so you form an evenly rounded cord (*figure 19*).

TASSELS

Follow the project directions regarding the exact length and number of strands; one strand should be longer than the others. Insert a large crochet hook into the stitch in which a tassel is to be inserted. Draw one end of the cut strands through this stitch, making sure that they hang evenly on both sides of the stitch (with the exception of one end of the longer strand). Wrap the longer strand around the others five times, securing the tassel around the stitch. Insert a small crochet hook up into the tassel, catch the piece of longer strand that has been wrapping around the tassel, and pull it through so that it hangs down with the remaining strands. Trim if necessary to even all the lengths.

About the Designers

TANYA ALPERT

Tanya Alpert is a Ukraine-born fiber artist, knitwear designer, and author of *Haiku Knits*. She graduated from the Kiev College of Applied Arts, Ukraine, and after moving to the United States in 1988 she worked as a graphic artist while designing and exhibiting her fiber art pieces around the country. In 2005 she opened her yarn boutique, Knitting by the Beach, in Solana Beach, California, where she began teaching and designing knitwear.

CYNTHIA CRESCENZO

Cynthia Crescenzo, camera in hand, travels and photographs everything knitted, gathering inspiration for her designs. Through her online store and blog, Cynthia shares her love of design and fashion with her readers. Her transitional pieces go from day to night—from lunch in the city to dinner in a cozy, country inn. She creates knitwear that is comfortable yet elegant, and right for any occasion. Visit her website: www.knittingcentral.com.

HEATHER DIXON

Born in Nottingham, England, Heather taught herself to knit at an early age. After graduating with a degree in knitwear design from the Nottingham Trent University, Heather worked in the UK and Italy before moving to New York City in 1999. After a couple of years designing sweaters and embellishments for Urban Outfitters, Heather decided it was time to run away to the country, where she could turn her hand-knitting obsession into her full-time career.

Heather now lives in a converted barn in the Catskills with her actor/artist/chef-fella and Lucky, the sweetest dog in the world. Her website is www.armyofknitters.com.

LISA HOFFMAN

Lisa Hoffman is a yarn artist living in New York City who has published patterns in *Vogue Knitting* magazine and in the books *Vogue Knitting On the Go! Bags Two* and *Vogue Knitting On the Go! Mittens & Gloves*. Fiber and color direct Lisa's designs, and all her creations are garments she herself would want to wear.

DANIELA JOHANNSENOVA

Daniela Johannsenova was born in the former Czechoslovakia. Crafts and especially knitting and sewing were always part of Daniela's life. In 2006, after some of her creations appeared in a German fashion magazine, she decided to open a yarn shop in the city center of Cologne, Germany—Maschenkunst—which has become extremely popular. Daniela's designs are featured in major German magazines, including *Verena Knitting*. She works as a knitwear editor at the family lifestyle publication *Magazín Luna*, where she creates 10 baby and children's collections per year. Daniela is the distributor of Artyarns yarn across Europe. Her website is www.maschenkunst.de/.

ANDREA JURGRAU

Andrea Jurgrau has been designing knitting patterns as BadCatDesigns for about 10 years. She specializes in accessories and lace and often uses small beads to embellish her work in subtle ways. She loves skinny, elegant yarn and little needles. Andrea has a BFA in design and technical theater. She lives just north of New York City and blogs at www.badcatdesigns.blogspot.com/.

JUDITH RUDNICK KANE

Judith Rudnick Kane has an extensive art background, holding a BFA and an MA in painting from Hunter College. She worked as a studio artist for many years and her paintings have been exhibited widely; she has taught art, color theory, and knitting at all age and skill levels.

Judith is the owner of Yarns for Your Soul LLC, in Manchester, Vermont, and has designed many of the models on display in the shop. Judith also does needlepoint and creates her own colorful canvases.

LAURIE KIMMELSTIEL

Laurie Kimmelstiel is a knitter, weaver, designer, and founder of The Ethelridge Road Knitting Salon. She is a contributor to a variety of knitting publications and co-author of *Exquisite Little Knits* (Lark Crafts, 2004). She chronicles her knitting life at: http://the-yarn-princess.blogspot.com; her website is www.whiteridgecrafts.com; and she can be reached at knittingsalon@gmail.com.

MICHELLE MILLER

Michelle knits tin hats and writes knitting patterns for knitters. Despite her best efforts, she recently obtained a masters degree in applied physics. Most of her time is spent keeping her four-year-old from swinging from the chandelier and her husband distracted from the constant influx of new yarn. Her website is www.fickleknitter.com.

ANNIE MODESITT

Annie lives, knits, and crochets in St. Paul, Minnesota, with her family. She loves to bike, and when she's not shoveling snow she's usually riding around her neighborhood. Annie knits in the Combination Method and believes there is no wrong way to knit! Her website is www.modeknit.com.

BROOKE NICO

Brooke Nico is from St. Louis, Missouri, where she is co-owner of Kirkwood Knittery and a mother to three wonderful children. Her designs have been featured in *Vogue Knitting*, *Debbie Bliss Magazine*, and *Knitter's Magazine*.

SHARON SORKEN

Sharon has been a passionate knitter all her life, for pleasure and eventually for a livelihood. Her designs are sold in stores all over the country. (Nancy Reagan appeared for a television interview in one of her designs.)

She now designs for Artyarns, a luxury yarn company. She works with the finest cashmere, silk, silk mohair, and merino wool, and the yarns inspire her designs. Find Sharon at sheknits@optonline.net and www.sharonsorken.com.

LYNN WILSON

Lynn is a designer, knitting instructor, and dedicated knitter. Lynn's designs have been featured in *Knit Simple Magazine*, *60 Quick Knits in Cascade 220*, *60 Quick Baby Knits*, and *Vogue Knitting On the Go! Bags Two*. She has designed for Be Sweet Yarns and Tanglewood Fiber Creations, and has her own collection of Lynn Wilson Designs knitting patterns. More information is available on her website: www.lwilsondesigns.com.

LAURA ZUKAITE

A native Lithuanian and a graduate from Parsons The New School for Design, Laura is happily pursuing her career as a sweater designer in New York City. She is the author of *Luxe Knits* (Lark Crafts, 2009) and *Luxe Knits: The Accessories* (Lark Crafts, 2010), books that feature designs made with exceptional yarns that convey Laura's design philosophy. Her website is www.laurazukaite.com.

Knitting Abbreviations

ABBR.	DESCRIPTION	ABBR.	DESCRIPTION	ABBR.	DESCRIPTION	ABBR.	DESCRIPTION
[ ]	work instructions within brackets as many times as directed	fl	front loop(s)	PM	place marker	sl1k	slip 1 knitwise
( )	work instructions within parentheses as many times as directed	foll	follow/follows/ following	pop	popcorn	sl1p	slip 1 purlwise
* *	repeat instructions following the asterisks as directed	g	gram	prev	previous	ss	slip stitch (Canadian)
*	repeat instructions following the single asterisk as directed	inc	increase/ increases/ increasing	psso	pass slipped stitch over	ssk	slip, slip, knit these 2 stitches together—a decrease
"	inches	k or K	knit	pwise	purlwise	sssk	slip, slip, slip, knit 3 stitches together
alt	alternate	kwise	knitwise	p2tog	purl 2 stitches together	st(s)	stitch(es)
ap-prox	approximately	k2tog	knit 2 stitches together	rem	remain/ remaining	St st	stockinette stitch/stocking stitch
beg	begin/beginning	LH	left hand	rep	repeat(s)	tbl	through back loop
bet	between	lp(s)	loop(s)	rev St st	reverse stockinette stitch	tog	together
BO	bind off	m	meter(s)	RH	right hand	WS	wrong side
CC	contrasting color	MC	main color	rnd(s)	round(s)	wyib	with yarn in back
cm	centimeter(s)	mm	millimeter(s)	RS	right side	wyif	with yarn in front
cn	cable needle	M1	make 1 stitch	sk	skip	yd(s)	yard(s)
CO	cast on	M1 p-st	make 1 purl stitch	skp	slip, knit, pass stitch over—one stitch decreased	yfwd	yarn forward
cont	continue	oz	ounce(s)	sk2p	slip 1, knit 2 together, pass slip stitch over the knit 2 together; 2 stiches have been decreased	yo	yarn over
dec	decrease/ decreases/ decreasing	p or P	purl	sl	slip	yon	yarn over needle
dpn	double pointed needle(s)	pat(s) or patt	patterns	sl st	slip stitch(es)	yrn	yarn around needle

Needle Size Chart

METRIC (MM)	US	UK/ CANADIAN
2.0	0	14
2.25	1	13
2.75	2	12
3.0	—	11
3.25	3	10
3.5	4	—
3.75	5	9
4.0	6	8
4.5	7	7
5.0	8	6
5.5	9	5
6.0	10	4
6.5	10½	3
7.0	—	2
7.5	—	1
8.0	11	0
9.0	13	00
10.0	15	000
12.0	17	—
16.0	19	—
19.0	35	—
25.0	50	—

Yarn Substitution Chart

YARN IN PROJECT	WEIGHT	YARN SUBSTITUTION
Beaded Cashmere & Sequins	4	Lion Brand Amazing or Glitterspun or Wool or Superwash Merino-Cashmere
Beaded Ensemble	4	Lion Brand Amazing or Glitterspun or Wool or Superwash Merino-Cashmere
Beaded Mohair & Sequins	3	Lion Brand Microspun
Beaded Pearl & Sequins	4	Lion Brand Amazing or Glitterspun or Wool or Superwash Merino-Cashmere
Beaded Pearl	4	Lion Brand Amazing or Glitterspun or Wool or Superwash Merino-Cashmere
Beaded Rhapsody & Sequins	4	Lion Brand Amazing or Glitterspun or Wool or Superwash Merino-Cashmere
Beaded Silk & Sequins Light	3	Lion Brand Microspun
Beaded Silk Light	3	Lion Brand Microspun
Cashmere 1	0	Lion Brand LB 1878
Cashmere 2	1	Lion Brand Sock-Ease™ Yarn
Cashmere 3	2	Vanna's Glamour™ Yarn
Cashmere 5	4	Lion Brand Amazing or Glitterspun or Wool or Superwash Merino-Cashmere
Cashmere Glitter	2	Vanna's Glamour™ Yarn
Ensemble	4	Lion Brand Amazing or Glitterspun or Wool or Superwash Merino-Cashmere
Ensemble Light	3	Lion Brand Microspun
Mohair Glitter	0	Lion Brand LB 1878
Mohair Splash	3	Lion Brand Microspun
Regal Silk	3	Lion Brand Microspun
Rhapsody Glitter Light	3	Lion Brand Microspun
Silk Mohair	0	Lion Brand LB 1878
Silk Pearl	3	Lion Brand Microspun
Silk Rhapsody	4	Lion Brand Amazing or Glitterspun or Wool or Superwash Merino-Cashmere
Silk Rhapsody Glitter	4	Lion Brand Amazing or Glitterspun or Wool or Superwash Merino-Cashmere
Ultrabulky	5	Lion Brand Wool-Ease® Chunky Yarn

Yarn Weights

YARN WEIGHT SYMBOL & CATEGORY NAMES	0 lace	1 super fine	2 fine	3 light	4 medium	5 bulky	6 super bulky
TYPE OF YARNS IN CATEGORY	Fingering 10-count crochet thread	Sock, Fingering, Baby	Sport, Baby	DK, Light Worsted	Worsted, Afghan, Aran	Chunky, Craft, Rug	Bulky, Roving

Source: Craft Yarn Council of America's www.YarnStandards.com

Photo by: Elliot Schreier

About the Author

Iris Schreier couldn't find the yarn she wanted for her designs and, with the mission of elevating the art of knitting, decided to create it herself. She is the founder of Artyarns, a company that has built its reputation on producing luxurious, sophisticated hand-dyed yarns of the highest quality. Since 2002, Artyarns has offered a variety of special yarns, including merino wool, silk, cashmere, mohair, and has featured fiber blends as well as embellished yarns enhanced with beads, sequins, and gold or silver metallic strands.

Taught by her mother, Iris has been knitting since she was about six years old. She has always been drawn to decorative and fanciful types of projects, and is known best for her unique designs for modular knitting, lacework, and reversible knitwear. Iris is the author of several Lark books, including *Exquisite Little Knits* (with co-author Laurie Kimmelstiel, 2004), *Modular Knits* (2005), *Lacy Little Knits* (2007), and *Iris Schreier's Reversible Knits* (2009).

Her original techniques are used in knitting workshops around the world, and her patterns have been translated into various languages. Iris has appeared on the television programs *Knitty Gritty* and *Needle Arts Studio*, and has written articles and published patterns in leading magazines. Visit her Facebook page at www.facebook.com/artyarns and see her designs on her websites: www.artyarns.com and www.irisknits.com.

Acknowledgments

Without the support of the incredible group of designers who contributed to this collection, it would just not have been possible to create this book. You are all terrific! My mom pitched in with last minute knitting and I really appreciate that, as well as the encouragement I received from Elliot, Owen, and Jason during this process. American Express Open and Officelab contributed to the Artyarns re-design, which was such a part of this publication. And many thanks to everyone at Lark who has pulled this together, including Amy Polcyn, Thom O'Hearn, Megan Kirby, Orrin Lundgren, Lynne Harty, Laura Palese, and most importantly my editor Valerie Shrader who will be missed!

Project Index